Dinner at The White House

By LOUIS ADAMIC

HARPER & BROTHERS Publishers
NEW YORK and LONDON

8-6

D-W

TO
GEORGE P. SKOURAS

Table of Contents

PART I

*A SINGULAR EVENING
WITH PLURAL
MEANINGS*

CHAPTER I

The Invitation

S HOULD like a chance to talk to you," read
Mrs. Roosevelt's telegram dated January 9,
1942, "and wonder if you would care to dine with
me Tuesday the thirteenth at the White House and
go to Philadelphia Orchestra concert at Constitution Hall, Toscanini conducting. Of course if Mrs.
Adamic cares to come too I shall be delighted."

"If I care to come too!" remarked Stella.

The next day, a wire from Mrs. James M. Helm,
permanent White House social secretary: "Mrs.
Roosevelt delighted you and Mrs. Adamic can
come to dinner on Tuesday, January thirteenth.
Black tie. Seven-thirty."

I was fairly sure I knew what Mrs. Roosevelt
wanted to talk about. In October 1941 I had
published a book called *Two-Way Passage* which
interested her. About a week after Pearl Harbor,
while traveling in California as assistant director
of the Office of Civilian Defense, she had mentioned in "My Day" that she was reading it in
snatches. Then on December 29 she wrote that

the book seemed to her worth while for the ex-
planations it gave "of the various pulls which our
mixed population has to undergo." But she
thought my proposal at the end contained more
difficulties than I appeared to realize.

The proposal—put in the form of a phantasy—
was that while Europe was occupied the United
States develop economic and political reconstruction programs for the various countries and teams
of carefully selected and trained people, many of
them first- and second-generation Americans with
backgrounds in European lands or regions, possibly including such men as Wendell Willkie,
whose father had immigrated from Germany.
Plans would be formulated and personnel held in
readiness to enter the countries the moment they
were liberated, fill in the vacuum left by the defeated Axis forces and help the peoples work themselves out of devastation and confusion toward
rehabilitation. I thought we must begin way be-
forehand to plan for the postwar period, as we
hadn't done during World War I.

America today was the result of a lot of immigrants in the past three hundred years making
the Passage Here; now, to keep the Old World
from blowing up again in everybody's face with
another war after this one was over, I suggested that
4 we make the Passage Back in person and, while

administering relief and reconstruction, convey as much as we could of our American experience in democracy—including the practice of federalism, the trend toward general welfare, the spread of ethnic "unity within diversity," and the principle of the importance of the individual.

Mrs. Roosevelt did not specify the difficulties she saw. On December 31 she returned to the subject, expressing doubt that my "plan could be carried out in exactly the way" I had outlined it. But she made it clear that the book was a pre-Pearl Harbor publication and she wondered how I might revise my "plan" now that we were actually in the war.

Between mid-October and the early days of December 1941 the book evoked considerable public comment, some favorable, some unfavorable, some mixed. It brought me over a thousand letters. But Pearl Harbor reduced the mail inflow to a trickle until Mrs. Roosevelt's published comments stirred up new interest.

I could not doubt that Mrs. Roosevelt wished to discuss *Two-Way Passage*. I had been considering how my idea would adjust to the new situation—our entry into total war.*

* To follow the ensuing narrative, it is not essential to be familiar with the full Two-Way Passage idea. For those who wish to know more about it at this point, there is a partial post-Pearl Harbor restatement on pp. 243-47.—*L. A.*

Expecting that my opportunity to talk with her would be very limited, I typed out some points I wanted to be sure to emphasize—among others, that the proposal was not a "plan," as she had characterized it, but an idea, a suggestion, deliberately presented in the form of a wishful phantasy in order to leave it wide open to the pressure of events and to continual revision in practical procedure.

Mrs. Roosevelt's invitation sent me on a spree of conjecture. Did the President know about it? Had they discussed *Two-Way Passage?* Had she summarized it for him?

I doubted that F.D.R. had found time to read a three-hundred-page book since Pearl Harbor and it seemed unlikely that he had seen it before then —and before his wife had read it. The military situation was grave beyond possibility of exaggeration; and one assumed, one hoped, that he was busy with it every minute of his waking hours

CHAPTER II

Seven-Thirty

TO MY telegraphed requests for a reservation, five Washington hotels replied one after another: no rooms. So when Stella and I arrived about six in the evening on Tuesday the thirteenth, we changed to evening clothes in the Union Depot's washrooms where several other people were doing the same thing. Then we checked our suitcase and sat in the crowded waiting room, glancing alternately at the afternoon papers and at the clock on the wall until it was time to go to the White House.

The war news was nearly all bad. The Japanese were approaching Singapore, winning in Burma; Tarakan, the Dutch Indies oil island off Borneo, had fallen; Malaya was falling. Our position in the Philippines was desperate. . . . The only glimmer seemed to be on the Eastern Front. The Russians and winter had stopped the Germans; here and there the Red Army was actually pushing them back.—

We happened to get a cab to ourselves.

"Which gate?" asked the driver as we approached our destination.

We hadn't been instructed on that detail. "I guess the main one," I said.

"Pennsylvania Avenue?"

"Yes."

The driver pulled up at the curb across from the North Gate; taxis were not allowed to enter the grounds any more, or even to stop on the White House side of the street.

It was a cold, crisp evening. Helmeted soldiers, bayonet fixed on rifle, walked post about every hundred yards along the fence surrounding the mansion.

In front of a small wooden guardhouse just inside the entrance stood a young navy officer, a tommy-gun over his arm. A second officer popped out of the guardhouse. We exchanged greetings and I gave them our name. They looked at us a long moment, then one of them bade us go up the curving driveway.

As we reached the portico steps, dimly lit by a large lamp high overhead, two men of the White House Detail of the Secret Service—tightly buttoned in heavy overcoats, hatbrims low over their eyes; short, shapeless, tough-looking—emerged from behind the great Ionic columns and closed in on the line of our ascent. They stood above us—an intent barrier.

For an instant as we went up the steps we felt uncertain, uncomfortable, suspect—until the men separated a little and the menace of their fierce interest relaxed. Stella said "Good evening" and one of them replied; the other, after squinting at me from beneath his bent hatbrim, stepped aside and motioned us to enter.

We hadn't told them our name. Presumably, while we had walked up the rather long driveway, the gate had informed the portico by telephone who we said we were. I could not see how they could be absolutely certain that we were we.

With this uneasy thought I followed Stella through the large door opened by a uniformed Negro. He bowed slightly and said "Good evening" in a low, liquid bass voice.

We walked into a spacious, brilliantly lighted lobby. There were several doors, a staircase, lamps on bronze standards, many pictures on the walls. Inlaid in the marble floor was the Presidential Seal, also in bronze, under an ellipse of stars representing the forty-eight states of the Union.

Another uniformed Negro servant took Stella's wrap and my coat and hat.

Presently a slender man in formal attire stood before us and, greeting us in an impersonally **9** courteous manner, inquired, "Mr. and Mrs. Adamic?" Then: "I'm Mr. Clark." I gathered he was the new Chief Usher, successor to the renowned Ike Hoover who had retired some time before.

He took a piece of cardboard from under his arm and glanced at what appeared to be a seating plan. "Mrs. Adamic," he said, "you will sit at the President's right."

Stella batted her eyes, swallowed, and looked at me with an expression in which were mingled surprise, pleasure, amusement and alarm.

I laughed, perhaps a trifle nervously.

Mr. Clark smiled. "You needn't worry, Mrs. Adamic. You'll be more at ease than anyone else in the room."

"Will I?" said Stella.

"Oh yes," said Mr. Clark lightly. "The person sitting next to the President always has the best time; he puts everyone at ease. And you, Mr. Adamic, will be on Mrs. Roosevelt's left."

—Why discriminate? I thought to myself, amused.

Mr. Clark waved us to follow him.

We were ushered into the Red Room, brightly elegant with white wainscoting and marble mantel offsetting the red curtains, upholstery and rug.

Three people were already there: two pretty girls and a tall, sunburned man of about fifty. Mr. Clark made the introductions, but neither Stella nor I caught the girls' names. They were about the same age, in their early twenties, and from their speech obviously English. The man was Mr. Robinson—Monroe Douglas Robinson, a cousin of Mrs. Roosevelt's, as we learned from "My Day" two days later. He wore a dinner jacket; the girls had on short black dinner frocks.

They looked at Stella's long dress and one of them asked, "When did you get *your* invitation?"

"Three or four days ago," answered Stella.

"*We* were called most unexpectedly only about an hour ago," said the girl, "and were told to come as we were."

Stella and I looked at each other, wondering.

Mr. Robinson had said good-evening in a quiet voice but now he turned to me with sudden vehemence: "Look, I've just come from Peru—this morning—after a long absence from home. What's happened? What's going on?"

I wasn't sure what he was driving at, what to say, how to meet his mood.

"What's the matter with the Japs?" he went on. "Are they crazy? If they're not they should have known they couldn't get away with a sneak stunt

like Pearl Harbor."

"Well," I said, "they made a pretty good stab at getting away with it."

Mr. Robinson did not seem to hear. "They're crazy, that's all. Else, how could they imagine they had a chance? We'll beat them to a pulp—blow them off the map."

Mr. Clark reappeared and invited us all to follow him. He led us across the lobby to a corridor and motioned us into a small elevator. As we rose to the second floor Mr. Robinson said, "What I can't understand is how—*why*—we were caught napping like that. Asleep at the switch! I can't understand, can you?" He glared at me.

The elevator opened just as Mrs. Roosevelt came out of a door in the wide hallway and walked quickly toward us. Her full-skirted black taffeta gown swished about her, enhancing the sweep of her movement. Her face was lighted with a smile, her hands were outstretched.

I had met her twice before in New York but tonight, here, she looked specially attractive, impressive. The upswept hairdress and the long gown made her appear even taller than she was. She looked well, strong, handsome; also sad, worried, almost harassed beneath her self-control. In her

left hand she held a small, silver-embroidered eve-

ning bag, and pressed against it was a folded piece
of paper.

The English girls, first out of the elevator, were
friends of the family; one, we gathered later, was
the President's goddaughter. Mrs. Roosevelt received them with intimate cordiality, then sent
them into the President's Study.

Mrs. Roosevelt evidently had not seen her
cousin since his arrival from Peru; she greeted him
affectionately and admired his sunburn. He followed the English girls into the Study and a
moment later I heard the President's familiar,
carrying voice: "Hello, Monroe."

Mrs. Roosevelt shook hands with Stella, then
with me. "I'm so glad you two could come," she
said warmly, earnestly. Her voice was much more
naturally volatile and less carefully modulated than
when heard on the radio or from the platform.
"This is a very special evening." She smiled suddenly and put an arm around Stella, who seemed
to disappear in a fold of her black gown. "We
haven't had cocktails before dinner since Pearl
Harbor but we're having them this evening—the
President is mixing them for us."

She strode with Stella into the Study. I followed. Through a half-open door on the way I
caught a glimpse of a large, well-lit room dominated
by a great four-poster bed—F.D.R.'s, no doubt.

CHAPTER III

In the President's Study

THE atmosphere of the oval room known as the President's Study—sometimes as the Lincoln Study—did not derive so much from the mixture of fine old period pieces and chintz-covered armchairs, the too-numerous paintings and prints occupying much of the wall space, and the cheerful, light-reflecting green-and-yellow curtains, as from its proportions and historic associations. I had heard the rumor (since printed in a slightly different version by Mrs. Roosevelt) that sometimes late at night when everything is quiet some of the White House residents imagine hearing in it steps like those of a very tall man thoughtfully pacing the carpeted floor. . . .

Franklin Delano Roosevelt, in his ninth year as President, seemed to be wonderfully at home in the room. About halfway down the long, curved wall on the right-hand side as we entered, he sat at a large desk. On it were a small ship's clock and numerous little donkeys, a cigarette box, ashtrays, a book or two, and a tray of cocktail makings.

A year and a half before—in July 1940, a few weeks after the collapse of France—I had been in the President's office with other consultants to his hastily improvised Defense Commission and, talking to us off-the-record for close upon an hour about the United States' ghastly predicament in the global arena, he had not looked well. His hands, gesturing for emphasis, lighting one cigarette after another, and flicking the ashes off his wrinkled seersucker coat, shook rather badly. The rings under his eyes were very dark and deep. The sharpest feeling he projected on that hot afternoon (at least to me) was one of tense concern crossed with resentment against men like Senators Borah and Nye who had obstructed his efforts to prepare the country psychologically and militarily. Several times, as he spoke impromptu with never any hesitancy and with what seemed to be entire frankness, his famous voice rasped with impatience at those in leading positions who did not perceive the nature of the crisis even after all the information at his disposal had been laid before them. . . .

. Now, five weeks after Pearl Harbor, there was no trace of ill-health, weariness or doubt. F.D.R. looked extraordinarily fit, self-possessed, relaxed— on top of the world.

He was giving the last few flips to the silver cocktail shaker. His face was ruddy and his close-

A Singular Evening with Plural Meanings

set gray eyes flashed with an infectious zest. He
had his head cocked at an angle of expectancy,
alert not to miss a thing, ready to make mischief
at the drop of a hat. He had just said something to
one of the English girls that made her blush, then
laugh.

That he was physically handicapped came as a
surprised afterthought touched by an instant's dis-
belief. The long, broad-shouldered torso and the
large head, set off by the well-fitted dinner jacket,
the soft white shirt and the natty black bow tie,
were powerful, magnificent, focusing one's attention. The movements of his arms and the rest of
his upper body were amazingly vivid and agile.

Mrs. Roosevelt introduced Stella and me to the
President.

"Awfully glad you could come," said F.D.R. The
pressure of his hand was firm.

Half a dozen people stood close to the desk
directly behind me where Mrs. Roosevelt was in-
troducing newcomers to those who had arrived
earlier, and for a minute or two I was unable to
back away. F.D.R. deftly poured the cocktails to
about one-sixteenth of an inch from the brim.
Then he suddenly looked up at me as though expecting me to say something.

"It's great to see you looking so well, Mr. President."

He smiled quickly. "Will you have a cocktail?" he said, handing me one. "It's an Orange Blossom."

"Thank you, sir."

The President glanced down. Fala had come from somewhere. I thought: Now the picture is complete. The Scottie sniffed at my shoes and the cuffs of my trousers, then sat back on his haunches. "You pass," F.D.R. said to me, laughing, "you pass. Have you a dog?"

"Two," I said.

"What kind?"

"Just mutts. But we think they're rather wonderful."

"Oh, I'm sure they are," the President said.

Mrs. Roosevelt turned. "Here's a letter from your boy Franklin," she said, giving her husband the sheet of paper I had noticed earlier in her hand. Franklin, Jr. was then serving on a destroyer somewhere in the Atlantic. The President put on his glasses and read the letter quickly, laid it on the desk, and blinked his eyes and smiled with a nod to his wife.

Meantime, slipping her evening bag under her arm, Mrs. Roosevelt took two cocktails from the tray and passed them to her cousin and Stella, Dinner urging the others to come up and get theirs.

at the   When we all had one, the President lifted his White House glass with a brief gesture of salutation to his guests and took a sip. He seemed to savor it.

My pitch of interest was such that I scarcely tasted what I was drinking.

"Fala is getting to be very famous," I said.

"Yes indeed," said the President.

"Last week," said one of the English girls, "I saw a picture of him on a magazine cover."

"I thought it was rather good, didn't you?" said the President, his look sweeping all of us.

We agreed that it was.

"Fala's been getting a better press than I," laughed F.D.R., reaching down to pat the dog's head. "But everybody misspells his name. There's only one l."

"It's an unusual name," remarked Stella.

"Yes," said F.D.R., leaning back. "One of my Scots ancestors way, way back was Murray the Outlaw of Fala Hill." He laughed again and put his cigarette holder into his mouth, tilted up at a sharp angle.

—Maybe an evening like this, I thought, is his way of keeping sane while in the dead center of an overwhelming insanity. Or maybe it means that, 18 since he is in on the inside of everything that's in the works, the day's bad news which I saw in the headlines half an hour ago doesn't worry him. Perhaps too his buoyancy comes in part from the great relief that our trance of indecisiveness is pierced and we are facing the showdown at last. . . .

Mrs. Roosevelt, going about with a tray of hors d'oeuvres, stopped to introduce me to her private secretary, Malvina Thompson, a woman with an easy, natural manner and a simple directness of speech. The President called her "Tommy."

A servant placed a bowl of popcorn before F.D.R., who said, "Ah—thank you," and took a handful and began to toss it dexterously into his mouth. His eyes caught mine watching him; and, staying his hand for a moment, he asked:

"How many copies has your book sold?"

"About twenty-five thousand."

"Really!" he exclaimed. "Random House has brought out my speeches and state papers in four volumes, but they haven't done nearly as well," he grinned, "though I haven't heard lately what the figure is."

—Just another author, I thought. . . . Good Lord! Has he read my book? . . .

"Let's sit down," said Mrs. Roosevelt to the roomful at large.

Following her lead and Miss Thompson's, we all *Dinner* drew chairs into a semicircle in front of the Presi- *at the* dent. I saw Mrs. Roosevelt reach for a rather heavy *White House* armchair and started toward her, but was too late.

"We'll save this one for the Prime Minister," she said.

"Is *he* still here?" I blurted.

"Yes, he's still here," she smiled, apparently delighting in my surprise which bordered on incredulity.

—Well, I said to myself.

Like most people outside Washington inner circles, I had assumed that following his Ottawa speech some two weeks before, Winston Churchill had returned to England. There hadn't been anything in the papers about him for well over a week. (Very few people had any inkling of his vacation in Florida.)

—If this isn't something, I thought, to see these two fellows together. . . . But if Churchill is still here, conferring with F.D.R., why—

I began to wonder. Mrs. Roosevelt had invited us. She had wanted to talk with me. What had happened? Why were the English girls called in at the last minute? Had Churchill just returned from somewhere? And had the plans for the evening been changed only that afternoon, and Mrs. Roosevelt hadn't felt free to cancel our invitation? For an instant I felt like an intruder, or rather like one who has been invited to this house but not to this room. I thought of the story about the woman in Carnegie Hall who went out during the performance for a drink of water, then got lost in the labyrinth of corridors and finally walked onto the stage while Heifetz and Rachmaninoff, or their equivalent, were playing a violin-piano concerto before a rapt capacity audience. . . . Or had Churchill been here right along, and was this dinner F.D.R.'s idea, an idea he had finally decided on only a few hours ago? If so, we were not intruding but on the contrary—

Through a kind of half daze I saw Mrs. Roosevelt sit down directly in front of the President and invite me with a friendly motion of her hand into the seat beside her.

"It will interest you, Mr. Adamic," she said, "that the President gave his copy of your book to the Prime Minister and specially requested him to read it. And I did too." Her earnest voice quavered in sudden mirth. "We're most anxious to know what he'll say."

When I resumed breathing I said, "Is he reading it—has he finished it?"

"That—we don't know," said Mrs. Roosevelt. "He's had it four or five days now—in his room."

"I'd give anything to know his reaction," I said, "—especially to the last part."

"So would I. And I think the President would too. He told Mr. Churchill he might not like the last part."

"Then my guess is that Mr. Churchill read that part first."

Mrs. Roosevelt was on the point of nodding in agreement, but she lifted her hands instead in a gesture which said: Who knows? We'll just have to wait and see—

CHAPTER IV

John Bull in Person

IN THE last part of *Two-Way Passage* I was a bit hard on the British. I pointed out what seemed to me imperial Britain's innate inability to play a constructive role in postwar Europe, which was bound to be very different from prewar Europe. And I maintained that the United States had a singular opportunity to help European nations move toward a democratic future. Our varied population drawn from many lands made us kin to much of the Old World. Our experience in political and personal democracy, our good will and material resources, our comparative lack of a record in European affairs resented by Europeans, and our distaste for the exploitation of other peoples were qualities which could contribute a lot to world stability and peace—*if* (a tremendous little word)—

If we could only realize wherein our strength lay. *If* we could distill a purpose within ourselves and recognize the nature of the opportunity before us. *If* we could during the war convince Britain and the Soviet Union that it would be wise to let us seize the opportunity. And, once it was grasped, *if* we could do a sincere, honest job of encouraging political, economic and social democracy no matter how far Left it might want to go.

I was sure of one thing: that unless the United States got a move on and managed to do something of this sort, however different it might be from the prewar brand of international diplomacy, the war itself was apt to be a picnic in comparison with what was loosely called the postwar period.

As I say, the idea briefly sketched here was presented in the form of a phantasy: Uncle Sam and John Bull talking alone on the deck of an American warship anchored in the fog off Iceland on a midsummer's day in 1941. John Bull, then in no condition to get on his high horse, had all the worst of the argument. . . .

Now, as most of the company assembled in the Lincoln Study were sitting and talking . . . as the President of the United States of America tossed popcorn into his mouth . . . as Fala sprawled motionlessly at his master's feet . . . as the whirl in my head subsided under the influence of Miss Thompson's matter-of-fact voice talking to me on my left . . . Mrs. Roosevelt suddenly rose from her chair and hastened to the door. And there waddled into the room John Bull himself, in person, alias the Right Honourable Winston Leonard Spencer Churchill.

Reaching for his hand, Mrs. Roosevelt said, "Good evening, Mr. Prime Minister"—formally, respectfully.

"Good evening, Mrs. Roosevelt," he replied, holding a long, fat, freshly lit cigar in front of him as if intent on making sure that nothing would befall it.

Churchill looked smaller than I had imagined him, especially beside Mrs. Roosevelt. He had a rotund, dumpy figure with short, slight arms and legs, narrow in the shoulders, mostly stomach, chest and head; no neck. Yet, as he advanced into the room, a semi-scowl on his big, chubby, pink-and-white face with its light-blue eyes, the knowledge of his performance since Dunkerque and something about his person gave him a massive stature. He moved as though he were without joints, all of a piece: solidly, unhurriedly, impervious to obstacles, like a tank or a bulldozer.

Behind him came a slight, pale young man, Mr. Martin, his personal secretary, and a robust officer, Commander Thompson, his naval aide.

"Hello, Winston," cried F.D.R.

"Evening, Mr. President," said Churchill, taking the dramatically extended hand.

For an appreciable moment the two men looked 25

at each other at once knowingly and quizzically.

What did their gaze mean? Roosevelt's expression mixed amusement and concern. But Churchill's interested me more, partly because this was my first view of him, but mainly because, with plenty of other Americans, I had long considered him dangerous: was F.D.R. a match for him? His large, round mug was perfectly smooth, blandly innocent —except for the eyes and mouth which were shrewd, ruthless, unscrupulous.

The newspapers and news magazines had had a good deal to say about the friendship between the President and the Prime Minister. They were obviously friends, but—perhaps less obviously—friends of a special kind, in whose relations the personal and the supra-personal were turbulently mingled. The divergent characters of their countries entered into those relations. Their own personalities were very unlike, in spite of certain similarities of background. There were tensions.

These thoughts rushed through my mind in a sort of shorthand, and I felt an overwhelming disquiet. Too much depended on the relationship between these two men. Churchill had arrived in the United States to visit F.D.R. on December 21. Their joint official statement, issued some days later, referred only to winning the war. But of 26 course they could not have avoided discussing postwar political questions. And there they would run into trouble. . . . Why had F.D.R. given Churchill my book to read? I had sensed in Mrs. Roosevelt's words that it wasn't all plain sailing with Churchill. What was the difficulty, the issue between the President and his British guest right now? Had they had an argument, a disagreement, that afternoon? Was Roosevelt putting the screws on Churchill about something and using my book and me to give them an extra turn? If Churchill thought F.D.R. was seriously interested in my idea, it would make for a lot of tension between them. It was one thing for me to have Uncle Sam tell John Bull where to get off at on paper; it was another thing for the President to tackle the Prime Minister on Britain's postwar role in Europe. . . .

Gazing at each other, smiling yet not smiling, they seemed to be feeling out each other's measure, speculating, challenging. A summation of personal maturity, a summation of their class, countries, period, with world-wide matters at stake, they were a pair of opponents naturally drawn to each other—terrific to watch. Each seemed to be saying inaudibly to the other: Now how am I going to handle you tonight? How will you react to my tactics? How will that affect our common cause, not so much during the war (that's all set) as later? And what do you understand our common cause to be? What about Russia? . . .

Roosevelt's face suddenly cracked into an open smile, which was at once sincere and an act. "Had a good nap, Winston?"

Churchill scowled again—or perhaps "pouted" is the more accurate word—and sticking his cigar in his mouth, mumbled something neither Stella nor I understood, although the room was very still.

Mrs. Roosevelt introduced to the Prime Minister and his secretary and naval aide those of us in the semicircle whom they did not know: the English girls, Mr. Robinson, Stella and me.

To Stella, he uttered an almost understandable "How'yedo," his cheeks bunched up under his eyes and his pout flattened into a grimacing smile.

"I enjoyed your Ottawa speech very much," Stella said, "especially the part about the chicken —'some chicken, some neck!' "

"Oh did you," Churchill beamed. He clipped his words, almost swallowed them; and his voice did not come out as full and clear as over the radio. His lips barely moved.

When my turn came to be introduced, I said, "Good evening, Mr. Prime Minister," and took his limp hand. Churchill mumbled some greeting or other. Our eyes scarcely met—through no fault of mine.

—I guess he did read the book, I thought; at least the last part.

"Will you have one of these, Winston?" F.D.R. smiled mischievously, lifting a glass from the tray.

"What are they?"

"Orange Blossoms."

Churchill made a face but he accepted the cocktail and drank it dutifully.

The Prime Minister sank into the chair Mrs. Roosevelt had reserved for him between herself and Stella.

Everybody else sat down.

"The man I just introduced to you, Mr. Prime Minister," Stella heard Mrs. Roosevelt say, "is the author of the book *Two-Way Passage*." She smiled to Stella.

"Yes, yes," growled Churchill, "I'm . . . I'm r-reading it." He stuttered a little.

He extracted a letter from his coat pocket, then said to his hostess in a warm, friendly tone: "Just received a letter from my wife. She thanks you, Mrs. Roosevelt, for the splendid gift you sent her." He put on his glasses and read her a paragraph.

"I'm so glad Mrs. Churchill likes it," said Mrs. Roosevelt.

29

"As for the gifts that have accumulated here," said the Prime Minister, "I lack words to express my appreciation. There are crates of eggs and oranges, and quantities of cigars and things. I know they must have caused a storage problem in the House."

"Not at all."

"Someone sent me a . . . c-corn-cob pipe," said Churchill and stuck his fat cigar into his mouth, making it glow.

"I received one too," F.D.R. said. "I get several a year."

"Is yours . . . w-worm-eaten too?" asked Churchill.

The President grinned. "How about a refill, Winston?"—lifting the cocktail shaker.

"No, thank you, Mr. President,"—glumly.

F.D.R. laughed.

From the hors d'oeuvre plate on the small table before her Mrs. Roosevelt took a tiny sausage impaled on a toothpick, and holding it out of Fala's reach as a bribe, coaxed him to lie down and roll over. Fala went through the performance, then sat up to get his reward. "Good boy," said Mrs. Roosevelt, giving it to him amid general laughter.

"Good boy, Fala," echoed F.D.R., and the Scottie ambled back to the desk and plopped at his feet.

30

A butler appeared in the doorway.

Mrs. Roosevelt rose quickly and said, "Shall we *A Singular* go down to dinner?" She turned to speak to *Evening* Churchill, who was slowly getting to his feet; and *with Plural* somehow, helped perhaps by Miss Thompson, she *Meanings* distracted the attention of the guests from the desk without our being aware of it.

Within a quarter of a minute or less Mrs. Roosevelt was pushing a wheelchair with the President out of the room. None of us had seen him heave himself into it. I hadn't noticed the wheelchair before; it must have been brought in quietly by his valet through the door a few steps to one side of the desk.

The ladies followed Mrs. Roosevelt; the men followed them.

I was the last out of the room. In the doorway I found myself beside Churchill, who had been ahead but had apparently stopped to wait for me.

He seemed on the verge of saying something, but refrained.

So I said, "It's a privilege to meet you, Mr. Prime Minister."

"I'm r-reading your book," he said, "and I—I find it—int'r-resting."

"Thank you, sir," I said. "May I ask how . . . how f-far you've got into it?" I felt my own stammer, usually under control, coming back; and I   *31* thought:—Well, at least we have this in common. . . .

"About . . . half-way," replied Churchill. "D'you really think . . . there is a problem here?—" He looked at me.

I thought he would enlarge on his question but he didn't.

I gathered he was referring to the early chapters dealing with the conscious and unconscious reasons why, before Pearl Harbor, elements in the American population had worked—some quite patriotically according to their lights—in the direction of national disunity. We had not removed the causes of disunity, nor had we shaped any large, long-range national purpose giving strength and coherence to our unifying impulses. Without such a goal the disuniting forces, now in temporary abeyance, would probably rise again during the war, should the present dark period be very long or should the Allies be threatened with ultimate defeat. They would certainly take hold after the war. . . .

"Yes, Mr. Prime Minister," I said. "I do think there is a problem."

Churchill's mouth tautened.

"It may not seem so right now," I went on, "a month after Pearl Harbor, but the . . . the elements of disunity, of potential disunity, continue to exist. They will come to the fore again, if not during the

war then after it sure, unless we succeed now in harnessing ourselves to a strong positive purpose. . . ."

"D'you really think so?" Churchill said again.

"I do, sir."

The Prime Minister stuck the cigar into his mouth.

As Churchill and I reached the end of the corridor, the ladies and the President were in the elevator, all but filling it. Mr. Robinson, Commander Thompson and Mr. Martin stood outside.

"We're waiting for you, Winston," said the President, smiling. "Come in, come in; there's room for you. The rest of you boys," he laughed, waving to us, "walk down."

Mrs. Roosevelt drew Stella and one of the English girls close to her to make room for the Prime Minister, who took the glowing cigar out of his mouth and entered the elevator with a cautious step. As the door closed he turned to the President, and the two men (Stella told me afterwards) gazed at each other again all the way down.

As for "the rest of us boys" descending the stairs, Mr. Robinson tackled Commander Thompson on the riddle of Pearl Harbor; Mr. Martin and I just naturally had nothing to say to each other.

When we got down Mrs. Roosevelt and the Prime
Dinner Minister, the English girls, and Miss Thompson
at the and Stella stood grouped in the lobby. We joined
White House them and listened to the First Lady telling who was
who in the pictures on the walls.

(On the train going home that night it occurred
to Stella and me that Mrs. Roosevelt had held
Churchill and the ladies in the hall both to wait
for the rest of us and to give the President, whom
an attendant had wheeled from the elevator into
the dining room, a chance to switch from the
wheelchair to his seat at the table.)

CHAPTER V

"Well, We Had a Big Day . . ."

MRS. ROOSEVELT, the Prime Minister by her side, led us into the private dining room—a relatively small, square room. She took the high-backed mahogany chair opposite the President, halfway down one side of the large oval table with its centerpiece of red carnations in a big silver bowl directly under the chandelier.

Churchill was helped into the seat at Mrs. Roosevelt's right. F.D.R. welcomed Stella to his right and his English goddaughter to his left. I sat between Mrs. Roosevelt and Miss Thompson, who smiled generously when, glancing at the silver service, the wine and champagne glasses, and the tiny vessels filled with cashew nuts, I remarked brilliantly: "Quite a party." The other English girl, Mr. Robinson, Commander Thompson and Mr. Martin filled in around the two ends of the table.

With the host and hostess the party numbered eleven.

Serving, by a staff of four, began almost at once. But as course followed course I had no very lucid idea of the menu, except that it was English. Later

Stella described it as good—thick broth, broiled fish, rare roast beef with Yorkshire pudding and gravy, string beans, salad, a trifle, coffee, wine, champagne, brandy.

F.D.R. opened the conversation the moment we were all in our places. He rubbed his hands, grinned and, looking over the centerpiece at his wife, said, "Well, we had a big day today."

"You did, Franklin?" said Eleanor Roosevelt, unfolding her napkin.

"And a fine press conference too," beamed the President.

"What did you do today?"

"I made Donald Nelson head of all war production with full authority and responsibility."

Mrs. Roosevelt nodded her approval. I thought: It's about time! For weeks there had been a strong popular demand that the President put war production under a single able man; Mr. Nelson's name had been prominently mentioned in the press and over the air, and his record and qualifications discussed.

"The announcement was given out this evening," added the President, well pleased with himself, glancing around the table for general approbation.

36 "Who's Donald Nelson?" asked Mr. Robinson.

Suppressed amusement flitted across several faces, including Mrs. Roosevelt's.

For an instant the President's expression was a study in incredulity, then he gave a short laugh, realizing the question came from his wife's cousin who had been in Peru for a long time, away from American papers and broadcasts. He laid down his soup spoon and told in considerable detail what a good man Donald Nelson was: how successful he had been as general manager of Sears, Roebuck, how highly he was regarded by industrialists and businessmen.

"At the press conference," the President went on, "the Wickard-Henderson rumpus was put to rest. The newspapers had misunderstood the whole business as to whether Wickard or Henderson had the final authority in the matter."

I did not recall seeing anything in the press about it, and F.D.R. did not explain.

"Wickard never had any intention of resigning," he continued. "The thing was mostly worked up by the papers. But now it's all straightened out." He took a spoonful of broth.

—Just like any successful, expansive American who on sitting down to dinner at home likes to tell his family and guests the things he did that day, sure they will appreciate what excellent judgment he exercised. . . .

Miss Thompson's eyes met mine. She was smiling.

I said, "This is a bit more than we expected when the invitation arrived. We expected to dine only with Mrs. Roosevelt and, I imagined, you, and then go to the concert."

"I believe it was planned that way originally," said Miss Thompson. "We're still going to the concert. It begins at nine. I'm supposed to watch the time"—glancing at her wrist—"so we won't be late."

Mrs. Roosevelt turned to me, hostess-like, but did not say anything.

"The President looks wonderfully well," I said.

"Yes," she said. "He's been very well of late. You know, we were rather worried about him a while ago. Every now and then he would suddenly develop two or three degrees of fever. The doctors could not diagnose it and then they discovered that milk was the cause. He's been fine since he stopped drinking it."

Across the table the President was talking to Stella in a low, serious voice:

"I read your husband's book. There's been a good deal of discussion of it around here, particularly as to which part is better, more valuable. Some people seem to like the first part best. But I like the last part. It has something. It has something," he repeated, gesturing with his hand as though shaping the thought and groping for the words which followed. "It opens vistas—it's an idea that really opens vistas." He gestured again, but with a different motion—as if pushing out into unknown spaces. "It appeals to the imagination."

Stella's heart was bounding. Now she grew numb, watching his face. It turned heavy, very serious and still, almost masklike as he lowered his eyes for an instant. Then he looked up again and smiled quickly.

"Will you tell that to your husband?" he said, the smile gone again. "Tell him that *I* like the *last* part of the book."

"Yes, Mr. President."

CHAPTER VI

Concerning the Aliens

"FRANKLIN," said Eleanor Roosevelt in a specially high-pitched voice, "we've simply got to do something about the alien situation. People are being hounded and persecuted. Reports of so many instances of injustice are coming in, it's upsetting. We've simply got to do something."

F.D.R. looked at his wife, at Churchill, then at me. The alien problem evidently was something he had not touched on in the office that day.

Churchill—whom I could not see, on the other side of Mrs. Roosevelt—mumbled a question which led her to give him some statistics on the unnaturalized foreign-born in the United States.

"About a million of them," she said, "are German, Italian and Japanese subjects—mostly German and Italian—whom we now call enemy aliens. Some are dangerous of course and the Department of Justice is attending to them; most of them, however—a very great majority, I am satisfied—are loyal to the United States and a special asset just now as part of our manpower."

"It may interest you to know what we did in

Great Britain," said the Prime Minister. He did not know the exact number of German and Italian aliens in the British Isles when the war began in 1939 and of course he realized the alien problem there did not approach ours in magnitude. "But I presume you will need to do what we did. We simply separated the goats from the sheep, interned the goats and used the sheep."

The President listened intently.

Mrs. Roosevelt frowned—possibly at Churchill's choice of words. "Just now," she said in an even voice, "one of our concerns in the Office of Civilian Defense is to forestall the spread of unjust suspicion. We don't want any witch-hunts such as we had during the last war. Once that sort of thing starts, there may be no stopping it."

"What do you think about this, Mr. Adamic?" asked F.D.R.

I said I thought the alien was less of a problem than the attitude of the rest of the population toward the alien, and that one way of averting causeless suspicion would be to give the country some idea how useful most of them were.

The President looked at me as though asking me to go on.

I agreed with Mrs. Roosevelt that it was important to prevent anti-alien hysteria. If it developed it would probably reach to the naturalized foreign-born. This would not only cut down production and retard the war effort, but might lessen the likelihood of our achieving a successful working attitude toward the rest of the world.

The President nodded vigorously. "About a week ago I gave out a statement urging employers not to fire aliens simply because they were aliens, or citizens with so-called foreign names because of such names. You see, Winston," he turned to Churchill, "we have a great variety of people in this country. Take almost any football team. Most of the players have Polish, Yugoslav, Scandinavian, Slovak names—even on the Notre Dame team which is called 'the Fighting Irish.' " He laughed. "And what is true of football is true of our industry. It is the immigrant from Poland or Germany or Bohemia or Italy or Ireland or the Balkans, or it is the immigrant's son, born here, who mans the machines and gets the coal out of the mines."

Churchill said nothing.

The President gestured for me to continue.

I said that a large proportion of aliens, I didn't know exactly how large, were people in their sixties and seventies—ex-peasants from various European countries with little or no education who were traditionally afraid of any contact with the government, any government. They had lived and worked in the United States most of their lives, and were parents and grandparents of millions of native Americans.

"We've been aware of those old people for several years," the President said. "I've had the Attorney-General look into the possibility of naturalizing them. One idea some time ago was to make them citizens by Presidential proclamation; another, by asking Congress to pass a law. I doubt if we can do anything definite about it immediately, but something will have to be done after the war."

I expressed concern over the hysteria on the Pacific Coast directed against Japanese immigrants and their American-born children. I knew that some Japanese aliens and even some few of their American-born sons and daughters (the Nisei) were anti-American, probably some very few were agents of the Japanese government. But I believed that, like the actual and potential Nazi and Fascist agents in the German and Italian groups, in fact, in all other American groups, they were the special concern of the F.B.I. and Naval and Military Intelligence. I had met many Nisei on the Pacific Coast, some of whom had written to me since Pearl Harbor; and I was sure the biggest majority, in common with the majority of second-generation German and Italian Americans, were loyal Americans. I thought it would be a serious mistake to

43

handle the Japanese element on the West Coast any differently from the way we meant to handle the German and Italian elements in New York, say, or Boston.

I had reason to believe that the hysterical cry in California, Oregon and Washington for internment of all people with Japanese faces, whether aliens or citizens, was stimulated by chauvinistic groups and newspapers, that special agricultural interests on the Coast desired to eliminate Japanese farmers and truck gardeners. And I thought it would be wrong to yield to such a demand.

"But some of the Japanese on the Coast *have* been caught as spies of the Japanese government," said Mrs. Roosevelt sharply.

The tone and finality of her words surprised me.

The President looked thoughtful but said nothing. Was he under pressure from the West Coast members of Congress? Was he obliged to heed Lieutenant-General John L. DeWitt in San Francisco? The general, faced with a potential military problem, was disposed to listen to the pressure groups out West who were taking advantage of the war to stir up hysteria. Had that hysteria touched Mrs. Roosevelt during her recent visit to California? Was she too under pressure? Were Westbrook Pegler's continual attacks upon her work in the Office of Civilian Defense affecting her? . . .

The manner in which she began this discussion was at odds with the content and tone of the state- <figure/> *A Singular* ment with which she closed it. At least it seemed *Evening* to me she was closing it. Was it perhaps troubling *with Plural* her so much that she did not want to burden the *Meanings* dinner party with it, and yet had not been quite able to keep it to herself?

The chances are that the decision to evacuate the Japanese aliens and Japanese Americans from the Coast—virtually to put them into concentration camps—had already been made.

(A month and a half later I went to California for several weeks. The evacuation of the Japanese and Japanese Americans was in progress. General De-Witt's order to evacuate them, authorized by the President as Commander-in-Chief, was posted on walls, on tree trunks, on telephone poles—one of the most un-American documents ever issued in compliance with a Presidential directive. I visited the Santa Anita "evacuation center" near Los Angeles. It was surrounded by a high barbed-wire fence and machine-gun towers. Several of my friends, natives of the United States, were inside. They asked me: Did President Roosevelt really want this? Did Mrs. Roosevelt know about it and understand what it meant? . . .

(The Japanese and Japanese Americans were   *45*

not evacuated from Hawaii, which is a good deal closer to Japan than California or Oregon. Why did Roosevelt order their uprooting on the Coast? All one can do is to call it a blunder—a detail within an overwhelming situation, but perhaps the Roosevelt administration's greatest specific blunder during World War II. I have been able to find only this extenuation—a weak one: perhaps the evacuation was consented to by the President partly because the military outlook early in 1942 was so uncertain, but mainly to protect the Japanese Americans and their alien parents from the hysteria on the Coast. Perhaps the Administration, absorbed with the burden of carrying on the war, felt itself powerless against that irrational frenzy.)

CHAPTER VII

Roosevelt and Churchill

CHAMPAGNE was poured.

Churchill told Roosevelt he had just received a cable from the British Ambassador to Brazil informing him that Sumner Welles (then Under-Secretary of State) had been given an enthusiastic reception on his arrival in Rio de Janeiro that afternoon.

The President acknowledged the news with an appreciative nod.

"What about Argentina?" asked Mr. Robinson, over to the left of the President.

"What about it, Monroe?" said F.D.R. "You've just come from that part of the world."

"I wasn't in Argentina, Franklin," said Mr. Robinson. "In Peru the impression is rather widespread that Argentina is Nazi—pro-Nazi, at any rate."

"We're apt to run into difficulties there," said F.D.R.

"Smoke them out, Mr. President," said Churchill emphatically. "Smoke them out now; then if they

47

turn out to be Nazi, you will know what they are
and how to deal with them."

Roosevelt looked at Churchill speculatively but
made no comment.

—Is he reflecting, I wondered, on the fact that British interests, backed by their government, have a strong influence on the politics of Argentina? . . .

"I heard a lot of talk about democracy in South America," said Mr. Robinson. "But just how much democracy do you suppose there is in those countries with their dictators?" He addressed the President, who was lost in thought.

"What did you say, Monroe?" he asked.

"I was saying that democracy in South America—"

"Democracy in South America," said the President, smiling, "—why, it's a fetish. Just a fetish. I was down there: visited Vargas in Brazil. Wonderful people, the Brazilians; they gave me a grand reception. In this country when we make a big to-do over a visitor, we throw confetti and ticker tape and torn telephone books. Down in South America they throw flowers, tons of them; roses, carnations, even orchids. . . . Vargas met me at the quay in Rio and we got in an open car and drove through the city. For miles the streets were lined with people, and the windows and balconies were
full of them, all throwing flowers and shouting

'*Viva la democracia! Viva Roosevelt!*'—as though
the two were synonymous."

"Friend of the underdog," muttered Churchill
with derisive condescension.

Laughing, Roosevelt continued: "And as we
rode along Vargas leaned over to me and said,
'Perhaps you've heard that I am a dictator.'—I
leaned over to him and said, 'Perhaps you've heard
that I am one too.'—"

Laughter.

Roosevelt said, "Then Vargas said to me, 'But *I*
really am.' "

More laughter, the President joining in.

"And of course Vargas is a dictator," F.D.R. went
on. "He told me why he thought only a more or
less dictatorial form of government was possible in
Brazil. I forget the percentage of illiteracy but it is
very high; and things are pretty backward in some
other respects. To bring about progress, Vargas
said, he had to be a dictator for the people's own
good. Of course it's always 'for the people's own
good.' I assume no one will think I favor dictators
of any kind, but—to be realistic—there are dictators and dictators. And I don't mean to suggest,
Monroe, that the people of a country like Brazil
don't believe in democracy. They do—passionately,
as they believe in everything else they believe in.
They make a fetish of it."

I remarked that in his Columbus Day speech in

1940, when he was running for re-election, he had used the phrase *"Viva la democracia!"*

"Yes," said F.D.R., "I did. Those are almost the only Spanish words I know—or rather Portuguese—but in that Columbus speech of course they were Italian." He laughed.

The waiters were removing the main-course plates and refilling the champagne glasses.

Someone asked if any of us had seen the sculpture exhibit of the Brazilian Ambassador's wife. Mrs. Roosevelt said she had and that it was very good. Miss Thompson asked me if I had noticed the reproduction of one of the statues in that morning's New York *Times*. I hadn't.

Churchill said he had met the Latin-American ambassadors and ministers in Washington, but had to confess that he could not tell them apart, and he wanted to know if Roosevelt knew, say, the Uruguayan Minister from the Ecuadorian one. The President conceded it wasn't easy.

With the salad came a little flurry of talk between those sitting next to each other.

Then the President's eyes circled the table again. "This afternoon I got an idea about what to do with Nathan Straus. A brilliant idea."

"I'm sure," said Churchill.

F.D.R. grinned.

Mrs. Roosevelt shook her head, smiling at Stella as much as to say: These boys!

"Let me tell you about it, Winston," said the President. "Nathan Straus is one of our fine Jewish Americans. He belongs to a well-known family and is a splendid executive. He did a grand job in Federal Housing but recently he resigned over something that came up—politics. I want to keep him in the government if at all possible—if I can induce him to take another job—and this afternoon I got the idea of putting him in charge of all the internee and prisoner-of-war camps in this country. A Jew in charge of German prisoners —won't Hitler just love that." He glanced around one end of the table, then the other, to see our reaction.

One or two of the guests said they liked the idea.

Churchill asked, "Didn't the mayor of New York, or his police commissioner, do something similar a year or two ago?"

"Oh, yes," conceded F.D.R. after a moment's thought. "I remember Fiorello put a Jewish police captain in charge of a detail assigned to guard the German consul-general in New York."

"Is this Nathan Straus idea for publication?"
asked Mr. Robinson.

"No, not yet, Monroe," said the President. "It has to be looked at some more. It may be *too* brilliant." He smiled at Churchill. "Besides, we haven't got any German prisoners-of-war to speak of. But we'll have plenty of them' soon."

"Winston," said F.D.R., "I've just thought of it: someone sent me a painting of you. It's by my desk in the office; I mustn't forget to let you see it tomorrow. The artist is a Canadian, a fellow from British Columbia, I believe. He sent a letter with the portrait in which he admits he's never seen you, but I think he's got a pretty good likeness— except that he gives you a little more hair than you actually have."

The Prime Minister of Great Britain rubbed a hand gently over his sparsely covered head and grimaced somewhat ruefully at the ravages of time and fate.

F.D.R. was enjoying himself. "There's a new portrait of me too. It's in the Cabinet Room; have you noticed it?"

"Which one?" said Churchill.

"Now look here, Winston, there's only one picture of me in the Cabinet Room—it's not even
hung yet, it's leaning against the wall by the

window on the left as you come in from my office. And thereby hangs a tale. The artist has a considerable name in his country . . . which . . . is not one of the lesser parts of the Western Hemisphere," carefully, conspicuously omitting the name of the country. "But he turned out to be a rather —shall I say, curious fellow. In fact he gave us quite a thrill. His country's Ambassador endorsed his request for three sittings and I agreed like a Good Neighbor. I sat for him twice, a half hour each time. Then all of a sudden last week Ed Starling"—head of the Secret Service Detail at the White House—"forbade me to sit for him again. They had discovered that the man was a two-time spy, working for a faction within his country's government—and for the Germans."

A Singular Evening with Plural Meanings

Two or three people around the table gasped. F.D.R. swung his cigarette holder in a gesture which said that sort of thing added to the day's fun.

"When he came the third time," he continued, "the fellow was told I was busy and that I asked him to excuse me. He said the sitting was not absolutely necessary anyhow; he would finish the portrait then and there—and he did, in the Cabinet Room. Perhaps he thought it strange that two men watched him while he gave the picture its final touches, but the probability is that he still doesn't suspect what we know about him. We're satisfied the Ambassador had no idea of the man's real business. . . . The artist-spy left the picture, and it's an interesting portrait, better than the one of you, Winston."

"I'm sure," said Churchill.

F.D.R. grinned. "You really must look at it when you come down tomorrow. I'm supposed to be making a fireside chat; the hearth is not in the composition but one side of my face is flame-red from the reflection of the fire. I thought I'd call the picture 'Roosevelt in Hell' and offer it to some-body—but I don't know who'd want it."

" 'That Man' might be an alternate title," I suggested.

F.D.R. laughed.

"A few years ago . . . th-the Wall Street boys would have been delighted to have it," said Churchill.

A gale of laughter.

"As we came out of the room upstairs," Stella said to the President, "I noticed Mrs. Roosevelt's picture over the door—"

"A Russian artist did it long ago at Hyde Park from a photograph at my request," said F.D.R. 54 "That's the only painting there is of her. She won't

sit for one." Then to the table at large: "There's
a standing offer of a hundred dollars cash to anyone who can induce Eleanor to pose for a portrait."

Mrs. Roosevelt laughed and squirmed in self-
effacement, half embarrassed and half pleased
that the subject should come up again, and said
firmly, "No, I won't sit for any portrait. I haven't
time. I'd feel foolish having it done."

"Anyhow the offer stands," said her husband.
"One hundred dollars cash."

"In the mail on my desk this morning," said
F.D.R., "there was a letter from Carol of Rumania
—you know, the former king. He writes to me
personally in his own hand from Mexico—wants
to come to the United States as soon as possible.
He says something about wanting to head the Free
Rumanian Government Committee—or whatever
it's called—which was started in Baltimore or
Brooklyn, I forget where. He's in a hurry about it
because he wants Rumania in the United Nations."
Pause. "But of course we can't let him in."

"Franklin, don't say 'we can't let him in,'" cried
Mrs. Roosevelt. "If you won't let him in you know
who they'll blame. That Rumanian committee
will be passing resolutions and getting people to
flood me with letters protesting against my objec-

tions to Carol." She laughed. "Besides, how can you keep him out? Look at all these other royal persons here."

"There'll be a slew of letters all right," Miss Thompson said to me. "Mrs. Roosevelt got the blame when the Duke and Duchess of Windsor didn't come here after he abdicated, although of course she had nothing to do with it—they simply changed their minds."

"Well, we just won't let him in," said F.D.R. lightly.

"*Don't* say '*we*,' Franklin," insisted Eleanor Roosevelt, a giggle lilting her voice. "I have nothing to do with it."

Everybody laughed except Churchill. To Stella, his grin was like a gargoyle's.

"There is nothing to this Free Rumanian Committee anyhow," the President said. "It's Carol's own little idea; a complete fraud. If he comes here, all it will mean is that the night clubs have a couple of new steady customers, and that a lot of people all over the country won't like it one bit."

There was a moment's silence. Everyone knew what the President had in mind. Churchill looked at Stella. She smiled. He lowered his eyelids discreetly. A guileless expression spread over his face. Then his close-lipped voice broke the silence:

"A matter of matrimony, I believe."

Another gale of laughter.

Churchill's eyes opened coyly and twinkled at the President and Stella; his fat, pink-and-white cheeks pouched in soundless mirth.

"But . . . s-seriously . . . you know," the Prime Minister said after a while, choosing his words with caution, "Carol is really not a bad sort. I've met him several times in London. His son is like this"—letting his mouth hang loosely, which caused another burst of laughter on the President's side of the table where they could see as well as hear him. "Carol himself is intelligent and . . . d-dependable . . . within limits. I must say that I respect him when it comes to the question of his redheaded lady friend—Lu-pes . . . Lepu-rescu," deliberately bungling the pronunciation, "whatever her name is. In London he never accepted an invitation unless it included her. I find that rather admirable."

There was a pause. I thought I detected a faint odor of Rumanian oil in Churchill's praise of Carol, and wondered if F.D.R. did too.

"Well, he must have something," said the President with a hearty laugh. "He *must* have something to stick to the gal for fifteen years."

"Or she may have something," said Stella.

"Yes indeed," said the President, laughing even harder.

A few days earlier in New York I happened to
hear an attaché of the Yugoslav Legation in Washington tell how, late in the afternoon about a
week before, Yugoslav Minister (later Ambassador, now ex-Ambassador) Konstantin Fotich had
received a call from the State Department asking
him to please rush over to sign an important document which was to be released at five o'clock. When
he got there Fotich found a queue of ambassadors
and ministers. Like him, several of them had no
idea what the man at the head of the line was sign-
ing. An Assistant Secretary of State was in charge
and in dreadful hurry to finish the business in
time for release at the scheduled hour. The last in
line because of the *Y* in "Yugoslavia," Fotich
barely had a chance to read the document before
he signed it, making Yugoslavia one of the United
Nations. In fact in all the haste he dropped a
rather large ink blot on it.

Now, at the White House, following the talk
about ex-King Carol, Mr. Robinson and Commander Thompson and one of the English girls
were discussing some of the royal exiles—ex-
Empress Zita of Austria and her sons, Princess
Martha of Norway and Princess Juliana of the
Netherlands, and so on.

Somebody asked me if I knew young King Peter
of Yugoslavia, then in London. I said I didn't.

F.D.R. said that back in 1919 during the Paris Peace Conference old King Nikita of Montenegro offered him a decoration but he didn't accept it. "He was a delightful old codger—something of a scoundrel too, wasn't he?"

"I wouldn't be surprised," I said. "He regarded Montenegro as his private estate and ran it accordingly."

"He was a pretty gorgeous beggar," F.D.R. went on. "His Montenegrin uniform was embroidered in gold. And there he was in the hallway, passing out decorations. Beside him stood an attaché, a huge, handsome fellow in a uniform almost as splendid as Nikita's, holding a purple plush cushion; and on the cushion were three rows of medals—the Orders of the First, Second and Third Class. My cousins Theodore, Jr., and Quentin had a bet on that one or the other, I forget which, could wangle at least a Second Class Order out of Nikita. Well, to shorten the story, the upshot was that each got a Third Class, and he wanted to give me one too. By the way, what's become of Prince Danilo?" he asked me.

"I don't know," I said, trying to think who Prince Danilo was.

"Apparently he decided not to claim the throne after Nikita got in bad with everybody."

"Apparently," I said, doing my best to disguise

my ignorance of this chapter in Balkan royal history. "He must have known what was good for him."

"I suppose so," said F.D.R., and the subject dropped.

Someone else wondered how the Belgians liked King Leopold's marrying while he was supposed to be a captive of the Nazis.

Mr. Robinson mentioned King Zog of Albania: where was he?

"Zog!" cried Roosevelt.

The upper part of his body leapt up so that he almost seemed to rise. We all looked at him. He leaned over the table and pointed a finger at Churchill:

"Winston, we forgot Zog!"

Churchill puckered his lips as if to say: So what, or, as he probably would have put it: Well?

The rest of us, beginning to catch on, were barely able to contain our laughter.

"Albania is a belligerent on our side," said the President. He scratched his head. "I believe there's an Albanian Minister or representative here—we must get him to sign our little document."*

This brought the house down. Everybody was

* Later that week a five-line news dispatch from Washington, stuck at the bottom of page 18 of a New York newspaper, stated that the Albanian representative accredited to the United States had added his signature to the document creating the formula of the United Nations.

laughing aloud but Churchill and Mrs. Roosevelt; some of us, including F.D.R., absolutely roared. Mrs. Roosevelt was smiling, but looked embarrassed or disturbed. Churchill's face—lips tight, cheeks inflated—was red: a picture of gargantuan, held-in amusement. His eyes blinked at Stella, who watched him till tears of laughter obscured her vision.

Still laughing, I thought:

—Too much depends on these two men. . . . A couple of emperors! Their countries may have some claims to being called democratic, but what the American and British peoples don't know would fill volumes—and most likely never will. . . . This business surrounding the United Nations document is both stupendously funny and stupendously terrible. Yet I suppose it's the way momentous things get started. Maybe it's the only way.* . . . Says one emperor to the other across the

* "Mr. Roosevelt wished an inclusive description for their league of belligerents, enrolling all the anti-Axis nations," say Forrest Davis and Ernest K. Lindley in their book *How War Came*. ". . . He rejected the term alliance, however qualified. So the urgent matter rested when the President and Prime Minister retired on the night of the 30th of December, 1941. On the 31st, the document had to be prepared for the signature of the Allied statesmen.

"The name came on the morning of the 31st. Mr. Roosevelt was awake earlier than usual. Running over the alternatives in bed, he fixed on the phrase 'United Nations.' Its pertinent simplicity recommended it. Rising, the President went in search of the Prime Minister for his before-breakfast opinion. He found

Dinner
at the
White House

dinner table: "Oh say, we forgot Zog." It's funny as hell. But too damned personal, haphazard, high-handed, casual. What else have they overlooked? . . . Of course the conduct of the war is on their hands. They may be doing as well as can be expected. Perhaps they are doing extremely well. But—

the Prime Minister in his tub. Advancing to the door of the bath, the President hailed his guest.

"'How about United Nations?' he called out as Churchill brought his soapy head above water.

"The Prime Minister ducked again to rinse the last of the soap from his eyes, shook his head, and turned a dripping gaze on the President.

"'That,' he said, 'should do it.'"

CHAPTER VIII

"My Friend Doesn't Understand . . ."

MISS THOMPSON reminded Mrs. Roosevelt that the time for us to leave for Constitution Hall was fast drawing near.

Mrs. Roosevelt said something to the butler who was removing her salad plate, while one of the English girls remarked that Toscanini did not wait for anyone.

"I hate to come in late," Mrs. Roosevelt said, "everyone stares at you so."

Dessert and coffee were served immediately; a little later, brandy.

The President asked Stella, "Does your husband smoke cigars?"

"No," she said, "he doesn't smoke at all."

F.D.R. snapped his silver cigarette case open before her. "Will you have one of these?"

"Thank you."

He lit their cigarettes with the same match. He took a long puff and looked at the chandelier. Then he turned back to Stella.

After a moment Stella said, "My husband is

going to be terribly pleased when I tell him that
you like the last part of the book."

F.D.R. smiled with a quick nod.

"Perhaps this will interest you," Stella went on.
"In the first draft he had you and Mr. Churchill
discussing war and postwar on the American warship, but it didn't work out. He didn't feel free to
put everything he wanted said into your mouths.
So he changed you to Uncle Sam and John Bull."

"I see," said the President. "I think that was
wise. You know, my friend over there doesn't understand how most of our people feel about Britain
and her role in the life of other peoples. Our
popular idea of that role may not be entirely objective—may not be one-hundred per cent true
from the British point of view, but there it is; and
I've been trying to tell him he ought to consider it.
It's in the American tradition, this distrust, this
dislike and even hatred of Britain—the Revolution, you know, and 1812; and India and the
Boer War, and all that. There are many kinds of
Americans of course, but as a people, as a country,
we're opposed to imperialism—we can't stomach
it."

Stella said she had recently reread Joseph Con-
rad's short novel *The Heart of Darkness* and found
its picture of imperialism very repulsive.

64   Blinking his eyes, F.D.R. jerked his head in

vigorous agreement. "That's what my friend over there doesn't understand—these feelings we have over here on one account or another."

"The Prime Minister has done a good deal recently to offset them," said Stella.

"Oh yes," said F.D.R. "But with all our admiration for England and for him personally those feelings remain."

I had been watching F.D.R. and Stella; now, unable to contain my curiosity any longer, I leaned over the English trifle, the demi-tasse and the brandy before me, which I then completely forgot, and stretched in an effort to hear what they were saying.

The President suddenly lifted his head and flashed an amused, understanding grin at me. "Don't worry," he said with a wave of his cigarette holder. "Mrs. Adamic and I agree thoroughly."

I couldn't help grinning back. "What about, Mr. President?"

F.D.R. laughed.

"I'm awfully glad your book has sold so well," he said. "It just occurs to me I want to give a copy to someone else. You don't have one with you, do you?"

"No, sir, I haven't. I'll mail you one tomorrow."

"Don't bother," said F.D.R. "I'll send over to
Brentano's in the morning."
I thought:—I don't get it. He must know I don't
carry copies around to dinner parties. Is he play-
acting for Churchill? . . .

The President smoked a second or two. Then,
his face turning earnest once more, he leaned over
the table toward me. "I was saying to your wife
that my friend over there," inclining his head,
"doesn't understand—doesn't appreciate—doesn't
realize that most of us Americans have very deep-
seated feelings against England."

Pausing, F.D.R. took a puff at his cigarette.
Everybody was quiet.

Then he went on: "These feelings perhaps are
not very credible from the British angle; but they
are natural enough and justified from our angles—
our different angles. My friend doesn't realize fully
—really—what a mixture of races, religions and
nationality backgrounds we are, and that our backgrounds persist, and that that is important and
makes for all kinds of difficulties—"

He stopped, not completing the sentence. Had
he meant to say: "and makes for all kinds of difficulties to one in my position"? . . . Or: "in our
relations with Britain"? . . . Or: "at a time like
this"? . . .

66   His face broke into a smile. "Incidentally, while

English is my main strain, I'm also part Scotch and part Dutch." He looked at Churchill significantly. The Prime Minister sat like Buddha, a big cigar in his face. "That combination makes one a good bargainer."

Churchill moved in his chair, met Roosevelt's amused look, took the cigar out of his mouth, and said something in his stiff-lipped voice about "the Dutch" being the more "money-minded" of the two. Neither Stella nor I heard him clearly enough to be sure.

The President laughed at his remark. Then turning back to me, he continued seriously:

"The point, which I am having a hard time getting across to some people, is that many Americans are anti-British. Take our large Irish Catholic group: they are anti-British for what seems a good reason to them even if it doesn't seem good to others; it has to do with their old country, and it's an old story. Or take our German element, also very large. Their anti-British sentiment may be defined, with exceptions of course, as a leftover from the old rivalry for empire between Britain and Germany. Then there are our Negroes, who don't like the British color policy. Not that our race situation is any better; it may be worse—I think it is in some respects; but ours is not a matter of official policy on the part of the Federal government. And there are other elements in our population with special reasons for being anti-British. Some of the reasons go back to Old World politics, to imperialist rivalries, to the position of their ancestral countries caught in the middle of those rivalries. In varying degrees this is true of our Scandinavian and Balkan elements. . . . And as for us old-line Americans, why, most of us were born anti-British," waving his hand in a sweeping gesture. "Take me. God knows, and my friend knows, I'm not anti-British—now. But I remember very clearly that when I was seven or thereabouts, in 1889 or '90, and my mother took me to England, and we saw Queen Victoria drive in her carriage down a London street, why, I hated the old woman."

I thought:—He must have said all this to Churchill before. He's using me to rub it in.—

There was a slight stir around the table as people sipped coffee.

I said, "Those feelings were certainly evident in the mail I received during the weeks just before Pearl Harbor, and I can't doubt that they will be extremely important again after we and Britain are both out of military danger, or even sooner—"

"Yes indeed," said the President as I paused, although I had not quite finished what I wanted to

say.

Mrs. Roosevelt and Miss Thompson had risen.

"I'm sorry, Franklin," said Mrs. Roosevelt, "but *A Singular* we *must* go now." She looked at her husband till *Evening* he blinked in understanding and nodded. *with Plural*

All the guests were on their feet. *Meanings*

"You will excuse me, Mr. Prime Minister," Mrs. Roosevelt said.

Churchill smiled wryly taking her hand. In his left hand he held his cigar in the attitude I had observed before; as if taking every precaution that nothing should happen to the long ash.

Mrs. Roosevelt swept around the table and stopped a moment to draw the English girls to her and probably thank them for coming on such short notice. The next instant she was at the door, whe : a butler waited with her white-fox wrap.

Meantime Churchill had stepped aside and backed against the wall. His chubby face suddenly appeared hard, rigid. His right arm hung straight down by his side.

Full of a sense of a large experience which would take me a while to figure out, I went up to him. "I want to say again, Mr. Prime Minister, that it was a privilege to meet you." I took his hand which he lifted just a little.

Churchill's expression was one of complex annoyance. I did not know it then, but this was the Roosevelts' farewell dinner to him (the press later

reported that he returned to England the next
day, January 14). He hadn't liked it at all. I was a
bloody nuisance dragged in by F.D.R. and he had
had to put up with me. This was implicit in his
manner, integral with his whole personality as I
had seen it that evening. He muttered something
I did not understand. His half-closed eyes squinted
up at me, and he stuck the cigar into his face and
pressed his back against the wall.

"I wonder, Mr. Churchill, if you have heard that
there's been a change of premiers in the Yugoslav
government-in-exile in London?" I asked.

"I have not," he replied.

"I saw it in this afternoon's papers just before
coming here. General Simovich is out and a man
named Yovanovich is the new Premier."

"Simovich?" Churchill shrugged his shoulders.
"No damage—no damage done."*

"You think the change is all right?"

He shrugged again, disdainfully.

"Good-by, sir," I said and went around the table,
thinking:—Just like an emperor. Tonight he's dis-
pleased. . . .

* General Dushan Simovich, ostensible head of the Yugoslav
anti-Axis uprising on March 27, 1941, had roiled the British by
refusing, that week, to fly to Athens for military discussions with
General Dill, the British chief-of-staff; and from the British
angle—as well as other angles—he was encrusted with a multi-
tude of overlapping inadequacies. . . .

Stella told the President how much she had enjoyed the evening.

"It was grand to have you," he said. "I'll be seeing you again."

Mrs. Roosevelt and Miss Thompson stood in the doorway with their wraps on waiting for us two and Mr. Robinson, who, it turned out, was also going to the concert.

Stella was on her way around the table to say good-by to Churchill when she saw Mrs. Roosevelt and started to hurry toward her instead. But Mrs. Roosevelt waved her back, smiling, "Yes, yes, say good-by to the Prime Minister."

As I reached F.D.R., Mr. Robinson was saying: "There are several things the President of Peru asked me to tell you, Franklin. When can I see you?"

"Come to my bedroom tomorrow morning about nine-thirty."

"Okay. Good night."

"Good night, Monroe."

I said, "Good-by, Mr. President. Thank you for a very interesting evening."

Tilting his head upward, he pressed my hand. "It was fine to have you. Thank you for coming."

Mr. Clark was holding Stella's wrap.   71

"You were right, Mr. Clark," she said. "I had a wonderful time."

He bowed slightly and smiled.

"Were you a little excited when you heard you were to sit next to the President?" Mrs. Roosevelt asked.

Stella nodded, laughing.

"People usually are," Mrs. Roosevelt said, laughing too, "so I suggested that Mr. Clark reassure you."

Mrs. Roosevelt put an arm around Stella and off they went—across the Presidential Seal in the lobby, through the door held open by the Negro who had let us in an hour and a half before, down the portico steps—with Miss Thompson, Mr. Robinson and me in hot pursuit.

The ladies got into the back seat of the limousine and the footman spread a robe over their laps.

"What's your name?" Mr. Robinson said to me. I told him.

"You wrote a book?"

"Yes."

"What about?"

Before I could begin to answer the footman had lifted up the middle seats and Mr. Robinson and I were clambering in.

"I do hope we won't be late," said Mrs. Roosevelt.

72

"We'll make it," said Miss Thompson.

"I can't tell you how grateful we are that you came tonight," said Mrs. Roosevelt. "The Presi- dent has been having considerable trouble in get- ting the Prime Minister to grasp what kind of a country we are. I've tried to help out. I talked with Mr. Churchill yesterday and again this afternoon. He said we would 'conquer the peoples of Europe.' I told him I didn't think that was our idea over here at all; our people did not want to conquer the peoples of Europe. I explained that many Americans have strong ties with the countries they come from. They don't want to conquer those countries or any other countries, nor do they want to help in such a conquest. All of us Americans, or certainly most of us, want to get rid of the conquerors and set the peoples free—help to set them free. . . . I explained this to Mr. Churchill and told him that was why we wanted him to read your book, Mr. Adamic. Because it gave a picture of this kinship between many of our Americans and many of the countries abroad. The Prime Minister said he understood—but I don't think he does. Not *really. . . ."*

PART II

WHAT A PAIR,
THESE
TWO

CHAPTER IX

Toscanini Was Annoyed

GETTING out of the car, Mrs. Roosevelt paid no attention to the burst of hand clapping by the people jammed along the driveway in front of Constitution Hall. She rushed in as fast as she could short of running, the rest of us after her.

As we went through the entrance Stella said something to me that did not register in my head until later.

When we reached the middle of the lobby Mrs. Roosevelt had been brought to a standstill by half a dozen press photographers and as many women reporters, yelling instructions and questions at her. "I want your whole party, Mrs. Roosevelt—please get them together." "Who are they?" "What are their names?" "Did they dine with you?"

"Why should anybody submit to this sort of barbarism?" said Mr. Robinson.

But Eleanor Roosevelt took it all very calmly, and we were not delayed more than a minute and a half or two minutes. She quickly grouped us around her, telling the reporters Mr. Robinson's name and ours (they knew Miss Thompson of

77

course). And no sooner had the bulbs flashed than

she lunged on again, following the two ushers who had been waiting for her at the entrance and who, barely keeping out of her way, dashed up the runway leading to the Presidential box.

We were late; Toscanini would not wait. As we sat down—Mrs. Roosevelt and Stella in the front of the box, Miss Thompson and Mr. Robinson and I behind—the Philadelphia Orchestra had just finished "The Star-Spangled Banner" and the audience was settling down, filling the hall with the hum of subdued talk and exclamations.

According to the writeups in next day's papers, it was a capacity audience. "Everybody" was there —Vice President Wallace, all Supreme Court justices but one, most of the Cabinet; most of the Senate, a large part of the House of Representatives; a lot of brass; many members of the diplomatic corps, including Soviet Ambassador Maxim Litvinoff; Brigadier Charles Napier, military aide to Prime Minister Churchill; Sidney Hillman—

Mrs. Owen J. Roberts wore "a black velvet gown ornamented with golden nailheads." Mrs. Henry Morgenthau's "long white ermine cape covered a dark dinner gown." Mme. Loudon, wife of the Minister of The Netherlands, "whose cape was of

gray fur, wore a simple black dress ornamented

with a clip at the neckline." Senhora de Martins, "who was accompanied by her husband, the Bra- *What a Pair,* zilian Ambassador, wore a sleeveless black taffeta *These* gown cut very low in front and back, with a perky *Two* little bow at one shoulder, and a brilliant ornament at the throat."—

The program consisted of Haydn's "Symphony No. 99, in E Flat Major"; excerpts from Mendelssohn's music to Shakespeare's *A Midsummer Night's Dream*; Bach's "Passacaglia and Fugue in C Minor," orchestrated by Respighi; Debussy's "Ibéria;" and Richard Strauss's tone poem "Death and Transfiguration." But, in one columnist's opinion, the Philadelphia Orchestra had never played less well. The explanation was that Arturo Toscanini was not at his best. He was deeply annoyed with the audience, which was restless throughout the evening, more interested in who was who than in music. Chairs creaked and necks craned and people whispered: "Oh look, there's—"

Myself, I noticed little of this.

I could see about half the stage by stretching, which I did as Toscanini, emerging again from the wings, walked slowly to the center of the stage and stepped onto the podium. His movements were those of an old man until he lifted his eloquent hands.

Suddenly, through a kind of delayed action between my sense of hearing and my brain, I realized what Stella had said to me as we entered the lobby: "Roosevelt told me to tell you that *he* likes the last part of the book. 'It's an idea that opens vistas. It appeals to the imagination,' he said."

I suppose that in a way I heard the music, but not really, not so I would know or care whether or not Toscanini was annoyed.

—So *he* likes the last part. It opens vistas . . . appeals to the imagination. But why didn't he say that out loud across the table so Churchill would hear him? Or has he told him so privately?

—Okay, so it opens vistas. Does that mean he'd like to use the idea in some way? How? . . . Wasn't the evening perhaps merely part of a momentary conspiracy, with Mrs. Roosevelt in on it, to drive the point that we're a complicated country into Churchill's stubborn cranium? . . .

—What a pair, these two! Too much depends on their getting along. And there's the danger of their getting along too well, for too long. This friendship between them. This kidding which is partly a cover for the contest or whatever it is that's going on between them. How is it influencing their decisions?

—"Mr. President"—I suppose Churchill calls him that even when they are alone. Does he think he's so shallow an egoist as to feel flattered by it? Roosevelt must know as well as Churchill that it's *What a Pair,* not flattery, implying recognition of superiority, *These* but under the circumstances a subtle inverted as- *Two* sertion of Churchill's superiority. Of course English and American customs differ. Roosevelt calls nearly everyone by his first name and he's not altering his habit to suit English ways. If there's rebuff on Churchill's side, Roosevelt is simply ignoring it, and with style. At the same time they are "friends"—maybe even friends without the quotation marks. They fascinate each other. . . .

—F.D.R. must be self-conscious under his airy familiarity. Otherwise, why would he bring up his notion that being part Dutch and Scottish makes him a good bargainer? Churchill lays no claim to his bargaining ability. He just bides his time. . . . Or did Roosevelt mention his ancestry for my benefit, knowing I was interested in such things, and phrase it so as also to touch Churchill? . . .

—Churchill is the tougher, the more finished. A Tory from head to toe. As a man, more all of a piece than Roosevelt. No splits in him. Cold. Hard. Deliberate. Capable of *anything*.

—His behavior tonight is probably characteristic. He scowled, was grumpy, impatient, but in all likelihood it was the farseeing, controlled impatience overlying infinite patience. His history shows that he can wait, and without losing his goal or his interest.

—The way he looked at F.D.R.—

—His morality, integrity, honor are bound up in the empire system. A Tory-imperialist-patriot, he's prepared to do absolutely anything, regardless of any other code or notion of right and wrong, in order to perpetuate what he believes in as good—good for Britain, which right now, in the world's imagination, is identical with his name. His personality with its Kiplingesque hangovers encompasses the tradition and ethos of the British Empire, the Anglo-Saxon success in recent centuries, and all the blundering and crime that went with it. He can be simultaneously honest and dishonest. Honesty and dishonesty with him are two sides of the same coin. On points where he and F.D.R. differ, he's ready, he's waiting, to hoodwink him for the sake of what he believes in. That's politics, but it's also Churchill, this particular politician. In the course of momentarily saving Britain and the Empire he momentarily saved the world. Saving the world almost incidentally with one hand, with the other hand he's intent on holding it pinned down to the same circumstances that brought on the current crisis which gave him the chance to save it. . . . No, not "save" it; rather, afford it another chance. However, if the world is to have that chance, Churchill's imperial purposes must not have any future beyond being the beginning of the Axis' end.

—His behavior tonight . . . lying low, saying little. He was deliberately, ostentatiously unreceptive to the point F.D.R. was trying to put over: America's mixed population and its traditional anti-British sentiment. It isn't that he's closed his mind to a fact; he's too shrewd for that; it must be that he's already evaluated the fact, correctly or not, and thinks that in view of other facts he can dismiss it from his calculations. In his coldly realistic, cynical mind, power in the United States (in spite of the Irish city bosses within the Democratic party) is mainly controlled by Americans of British descent or their imitators, not by Continental-European Americans; is ultimately controlled on the top levels by people whose first, instinctive reaction when it comes to a showdown is like Roosevelt's: "I'm not anti-British—now."

—As for the Two-Way Passage idea, Churchill would think it utopian nonsense. His view of the United States is kept up-to-date by the British agents in this country, and by Sir Willmott Lewis, probably the most brilliant top-flight analyst of the American mind, character and politics, who's lived here for decades. No doubt from what these people

report and from his own habits of political thinking, Churchill feels sure that the idea would not
receive a concerted backing by Americans, that
even F.D.R., the great experimenter and impro-
viser, the seeker after ideas, couldn't—should he
want to—put it over substantially, nor any revision of it which would retain its essence. . . .

—It opens vistas . . . appeals to the imagination. . . . Churchill doesn't want new vistas opened.
Not the kind of vistas which would spell the end of
the civilization he believes in and is fighting to
sustain. The less imagination in the world, the
better, so far as he's concerned. He's out to conquer.

—Churchill probably figures that the vast
American industrio-military potential will develop
much as Roosevelt sketched it in his speech to
Congress and as he's been laying it out before him
in their talks at the White House. *His* imagination runs to this effect: that under the whip of the
Pearl Harbor humiliation Roosevelt and his in-
choate country will become an enormous de-
terminant in winning the war; that, saving ourselves, we will save Great Britain and the Empire;
but that when it comes to international politics
apart from war, Roosevelt and the United States
will be incapable of leadership. He figures that if
Roosevelt attempts to work out a foreign policy
calling for long-range national responsibility, the
84 demagogues in the Senate—true representatives

of a politically adolescent people now desperately
digging into their resources, cheering him, calling
him "Winnie," sending him gifts—will reject it
as they rejected Wilson's League of Nations.

—F.D.R. must realize that Churchill knows our
strength and weakness and that he means to
turn both to British advantage—the first to win
the war, the second to perpetuate the British Empire. But given the splits running through the
American people, what is Roosevelt going to do
about it? What can he do?

—Tonight he looked wonderful. Every outward, easily observable aspect of his personality
spelled confidence. But does the confidence run
all through him? Or is he so much of an actor as
to delude himself? He's a magnificent actor, but
not magnificent enough to conceal the fact that
he's acting. With all his spotlighting of *Two-Way
Passage* he was not convincing—he's not convinced
himself. Churchill is right: Roosevelt's position
as leader is horribly difficult. And of course the
nature of the American people is not the only
baffling factor.

—Russia? . . . Throughout the evening F.D.R.
did not mention Russia. Nor did anyone else. But
the two men must have discussed her. In spite
of terrible military reverses the Red Army is still
the chief asset on the anti-Axis side, engaging
some three hundred German divisions. It's push-

ing them back. Roosevelt has decided to send the Russians all the supplies on all the ships we can spare, and as quickly as possible. Churchill is all in favor and the British Navy will help convoy the boats. But the visiting Tory ideologist is also thinking something like this: It's good that Hitler has been bleeding the Red Army; but he must be kept from bleeding it white too soon, before the Americans collect themselves. Of course this is nip-and-tuck—we know too little about Stalin's situation. But if Hitler doesn't exhaust him before Roosevelt's support is adequate, and if the Soviet system remains a power in the world, then in the so-called postwar period, Churchill is thinking to himself, we shall use Russia to scare the Americans with Communism, with the rising Slavs. And the Americans—even Franklin Roosevelt—will respond. Seeing no other alternative, they will back the Empire. . . .

—That's the horizon, content and central point of Churchill's imagination. He's not interested in anything else. Given his character and point of view, there's nothing else that could be in the back of his head.

—F.D.R., on the other hand, is committed to the growth and spread of democracy. Whether his commitment is by deepest conviction, whether it is wholly his own or partly the product of years of influence by his wife, who seems anti-imperialist in the traditional American way, the fact remains that to millions of Americans and hundreds of millions of non-Americans Roosevelt is identified with democracy—which in essence should be anything but pro-imperialist.

—So when Roosevelt and Churchill tangle, the atmosphere crackles and the bystanders hold their breath. Tonight the air quivered in that dining room.

—"None of that, Winston, none of that," I hear Roosevelt say a couple of days ago. "After the war things will have to be changed."—"What d'ye mean?" scowls Churchill.—"I mean that the common man everywhere will have to get a chance," says F.D.R.—"Rubbish!" retorts Churchill.— "Rubbish nothing," protests Roosevelt (or Mrs. Roosevelt). "We Americans believe in general welfare; we're working toward it in this country. That's what the New Deal is all about. And we don't like imperialism and nobody can make us like it."—"Look, Mr. President," says Churchill, "that doesn't make sense. Don't imagine you can extend the New Deal to India or the Balkans. You can't set your WPA up in Greece or Italy or Burma. You don't know the 'common man' in those places. And—you forget Russia and Communism. Friend of the underdog! You can play that role here in these favored States, Mr. President, and I grant it becomes you. You can indulge in social work programs in the Tennessee Valley and in West Virginia mining towns, but not in Sumatra or Albania. Perhaps you may ameliorate the color problem in Mississippi and Harlem by being courteous to the Negroes, Mrs. Roosevelt, but you don't know the colored multitudes that confront us in Asia and Africa. . . . Mark this: we're approaching the Either-Or era. In the colonial world, in places like southeastern Europe, even elsewhere in Europe as well as in Asia, it will be either Red Communism or what you Americans consider our deplorable imperialism (and may I add, only we know how to practice it, however poorly). If we should let you chisel away at the Empire the whole structure would crumble. Then where would we all be? Where will you be without us British? What will become of civilization? Christianity? With all our flaws the Commonwealth and the Empire are the most considerable stabilizer in the world."—"I don't believe in that Either-Or business," says F.D.R. "We Americans are strong on the Middle Road and lately we've got into the habit of walking to the left of center of it. Naturally right now, what with Pearl Harbor and our crippled Navy, we're in a tight spot, but this won't last. You just watch our smoke, Winston; you just wait. A year ago your British line was that you might become a 'junior partner' or even join the Union as the forty-ninth state. Your agents here talked that way. Now you're tell- *What a Pair,* ing me that your Empire has to stay intact. I must *These* tell you that, from where we're fighting this war, *Two* empire is irreconcilable with democracy. . . . You're waving Uncle Joe at me as the only alternative. Either-Or indeed! We on this side of the Atlantic like to have more alternatives than two."—"And fall between two stools? Very well, Mr. President," says Churchill, "we shall see."—

—And maybe it's at this point that F.D.R. comes across *Two-Way Passage* and catches sight of "vistas." Is he hopeful Churchill may consider them? Hardly. He must know better. Beneath his buoyancy tonight there was concern. Several times his expression suddenly grew very grave, as though mirroring the gravity of a situation hedged about with difficulties, in which he did not see his way. Is that the real state of his mind? Was all the rest pretending, bluffing, sparring with Churchill?

—For my part, if this is the way things are between them, F.D.R. presents too many question marks to be reassuring. I prefer his wife's mood. Talking to us in the car about Churchill's Toryism, his "reconquering Europe," she fairly bristled. She was good and sore. She's anxious. Churchill worries her. Perhaps F.D.R. does too. The most striking thing about her is her genuineness. Roosevelt doesn't feel as strongly as she does. Is he sin-   *89* cere? *Can* he be? In his position, confronted by the character of the American people, can he be—ever —completely sincere? Way down in him in his serious moments he must be terribly baffled. What do his Four Freedoms really amount to? And the Atlantic Charter? To Churchill they are probably as utopian as Two-Way Passage.

—What's our deal with Britain? Is it all a more or less personal arrangement between these two men? Does anyone besides them know? Perhaps Harry Hopkins knows, and Barney Baruch; both close friends of both Roosevelt and Churchill. Will F.D.R., the great Dutch-Scotch-American bargain driver, exact a political price from Churchill for our aid to Britain? Can he? Does he want to? Or has Churchill sold him the idea that we are as dependent on Britain as she is on us?

—We're at one with Britain now. We must win the war. But will we, can we—will Roosevelt, can he—oppose Churchill's postwar intentions?

—From his angle and being the kind of man he is, Churchill is honest in his devious way, is logical and fundamental in his British position. Is F.D.R. working, groping, toward an honest, logical and fundamental American position—toward an honest, logical and fundamental purpose? Was this evening part of that groping? . . .

CHAPTER X

"Death and Transfiguration"

APPLAUSE . . . Lights up . . . Toscanini bowing, gesturing to the orchestra to rise.—

Just before the intermission someone had come into the box and taken Mrs. Roosevelt away. Now she appeared on the stage to make a little speech for the current Red Cross war-fund drive. While the audience applauded, Toscanini bowed to her and she to him; they shook hands, then he withdrew. ". . . Thank you," she said in closing, "and I hope that the giving and the knowledge of what it will mean to the people will make all the givers happy."

"What did you say your name was?" Mr. Robinson asked me after Mrs. Roosevelt left the stage.

I spelled it.

"What's the title of your book?"

I told him.

"New book?"

"Came out three months ago."

"What's it about?"

I tried to tell him, but made a poor job of it.

91

Mrs. Roosevelt returned to the box. Most of the audience below was looking up at her.

I glanced at the program. The title of Strauss's "Death and Transfiguration" caught my eye, perhaps because it was last on the list and I was anxious for the concert to end.

By and by the lights dimmed out again—

—If only Roosevelt will watch himself. . . . If only he hasn't got himself in too deep with Churchill already. . . . If only his own personal habits, his propensity for familiarity, his casualness and good humor, his dislike of saying No and being unpleasant, and the absence of a firmly set goal, do not trick him into serving Churchill's ends too well. . . . If only his Wilson complex, on which Churchill must be counting, doesn't get the best of him. . . . If only he'll not worry too much about his next re-election. . . . If only he'll work at overcoming the country's isolation psychology as he overcame its depression psychology in the thirties. . . . If only he'll try to evoke and muster and cultivate what is best in us: our trends toward democracy, human dignity, general welfare, our latent sense that personal responsibility is implicit in self-government, our belief in education and human progress, our generous spirit. These things are there, but they are mostly asleep, dormant. . . . If only he will try to make us see that our own democracy, even such as it is, can continue only if democratic processes— *What a Pair,* not necessarily exactly like ours—are got under *These* way in other parts of the world. It'll mean some- *Two* thing even if he fails, or if he succeeds in only a fraction.

—Does he really perceive that the biggest source of our vitality, largely untapped, comes from the great diversity of our population, from the fact that we are not merely an Anglo-Saxon country but an extension, through three hundred years of immigration, of Europe, Africa, Asia? Does he— can he as an old-line American—really grasp that that's what gives us our main chance for a success- ful foreign policy? Does he appreciate the fact that American idealism is extremely fresh and strong in many of our new-immigrant Americans? Does he see that these people ought to be sought out, trained, and used in special functions?—

—Our democracy here has to become dynamic and begin to go places. Or it will continue to shrink and, after we have helped to defeat the Fascists in Europe and Asia, it is likely to curdle into Fascism of some special American variety, in- cluding racism (Anglo-Saxon, anti-Anglo-Saxon, KKK, anti-Semite, anti-Negro) and general re- action at home and crass dollar imperialism abroad. Then the worst in American life will come to the top and submerge the good, and the sound people everywhere else, those who are struggling for a decent life, will reject us and turn elsewhere for inspiration and leadership. And we won't like that. At the same time, whether anyone wishes it or not, we'll be pulled into an ideological struggle at home and abroad and be headed for another international war which will be also a civil war in many separate countries. . . .

—Does Roosevelt *really* perceive—?

—He's the current savior of his country—saving it in spite of itself. A savior of the world. Or, rather —with his vision, seeing as early as the middle thirties that the Hitlerian upheaval is a revolution against the democratic process, and with his political tactics which at their cleverest have tricked us into Lend-Lease—he's given the world a chance to save itself. . . .

—Just a chance. And Roosevelt is a potential center of that chance. Has he got what it takes to become its true center—not only to beat Hitler, but to withstand Churchill?

—A very, very considerable man, no doubt about that. A political genius. A virtuoso in human and public relations. With his extraordinary personality, in conjunction with the depression and the international crisis, he's raised the Presidency to something new; created his own criteria for the office. His leadership has the quality of exultation. He's made government exciting. He's made it mean something to the average man, both in terms of economic interest and dramatic show. With him around things happen. He has the gift of words. And that voice! "We have nothing to fear but fear itself." It's one of those superficially simple statements that hit the bull's-eye, that carry conviction, illumination, reassurance, hope, because they touch the depths in people—the unspoken, very often unconscious things. Exulting. It was the first of the tugs with which he twitched the country out of the depression doldrums. . . . In him flourishes the typical American ego, boastful of our ability to do things, to pull off the impossible. . . . This matter of winning the war. His manner tonight seemed to say: Don't worry, it's in the works. If only he'll make the same connection between that ego and a postwar goal. Americans only pull off the impossible when they care a lot about what they're trying to do. If only he's sure what he wants to pull off with Churchill. . . .

—The issue between them seems to be: Liberation *versus* Conquest. But is it really? Churchill means conquest, all right; does Roosevelt mean liberation and no maybe about it?

—It's one hell of a situation. If Roosevelt comes out on top it'll be a miracle. But he'd better—too

What a Pair, These Two

much depends on it for him to fail. Am I expecting too much of him? Isn't it enough that he gave the country a chance? He's only one man. Yes; but his personality has such pretensions, and he has endowed the Presidency with such glamour and persuasiveness, that there's no other American right now who could get to first base. It's up to him.

—Is he genuine? . . . I mean is he as genuine in his personality and therefore in his office as Churchill is in his? At the dinner table tonight my feeling about Churchill, although I could not see him, was far more definite than about Roosevelt, across from me. Why was that? Churchill, whatever else he may be, is the real thing, whole, the complete man. Unmistakably so. A very great leader and—so far as I'm concerned, and because of what he represents—also evil. . . . What is F.D.R.?

—Although anything but a mass-man, he has something in his makeup, in his political tactics and strategy, that has hooked his name to the aspirations of tens of millions of people in the United States and hundreds of millions elsewhere. Something which induces Americans to re-elect him, which gives him immense world prestige. He's communicated something of himself to the country and the world. And now he's one of the chief foci of human hope. . . .

—Can he—does he want to—get a move on now so we'll be better prepared for the postwar sit- uation than we were for the war?

—Churchill thinks he can't. Moreover, Churchill will do all he can to hamstring him so far as the postwar picture is concerned. Churchill's main hope in realizing his permanent purpose, especially if the Soviet Union remains a power, lies in the postwar mess being confused, mixed up, as messy as possible.

—*That* may be the crucial point in their relationship; and it's negative.

—Roosevelt? . . . He's dropped much of the dross belonging to his social stratum, retained some of the gold, and acquired other gold in the ore of other classes and cultures making up the country. Or so it seems. He's shown signs of knowing what the twentieth century is all about and of being attuned to the interests of the man in the street, "the forgotten man," the workingman, "the one-third of the nation which is ill-fed, ill-clothed and ill-housed." He's forward-looking and forward-moving, highly ingenious. He may be well versed in the processes of history; geographically his outlook is world-wide. He certainly is sensitive and responsive to contemporary trends and tides in human affairs, to what has been captured in such phrases as "Little man, what now?" . . . "The revolt of the masses" . . . He seems bent on going along with those trends and tides.

—He's conscious of himself, of his own importance, of the elements of his power. Intensely so. He relishes power for its own sake but also wants it for what he can do with it constructively. But his mind tends to skirt fundamentals. The chances are he's skirting them, laughing them off, in his talks with Churchill about the postwar era.

—Although it sometimes looks the opposite, Roosevelt is no radical, no revolutionary. He prefers to patch rather than to replace. He's a juggler, a manipulator of imperfections, but on an epic scale, which occasionally gives the illusion that something basic is going on. This, if it's so, is a serious shortcoming right now, is downright bad. It gives Churchill a huge advantage. . . .

—Roosevelt is often daring, both when it is absolutely necessary, as when he put Lend-Lease over on the country, and when it is unnecessary— for the fun of it. Or simply in the course of events, as when he spent billions, then tens of billions during the depression. Perhaps this saved the country, gave it a chance, as much as Lend-Lease did; for without that pioneering in big spending we wouldn't be ready for Lend-Lease, couldn't think of pouring hundreds of billions into war. . . .

—Mercurial, unsettled, often superficial, American, F.D.R. is still feeling his way. He enjoys or gives an excellent imitation of enjoying what to most men more or less qualified for the job would be a terrible burden of responsibility. He seems to have tremendous resilience, tremendous bounce.

—He's the husband of a remarkable woman whose influence on him is deep, continuous. Her qualities are not even suggested in "My Day." Upper-class by birth, she's a good deal like a peasant woman. Big, strong, down to earth. Awkward at first glance, but if one studies her, really graceful, agile. Direct and not unsophisticated. Apt to be wrong here and there, she has common sense and purpose in the center of her mental and emotional makeup, and is endowed with immense energy and drive. Those large hands of hers, with that old-fashioned ring. They mean business. . . . I'd say she has passion, conviction, direction, breadth. She's out for results—not to enhance her own standing or her own ego, but because she believes the results she's after are the right ones. She's been working on F.D.R. for years. . . .

—He can be worked on. His makeup is fluid. No part of him is deeply rooted in anything as old, formed, definite, rigidly organized as Britain and her Empire. He comes out of the American tradition—a newer thing, charged with the energy of a youth who has not reached full growth, who is still in process, still changing, still open to discovery and to new ideas; who is scattered, unformed. That's the hell of it right now. Where Churchill has found an absolute answer, Roosevelt is still probing, asking questions. Where Churchill gains strength from the single-mindedness of his inner core of belief, Roosevelt's strength is divided against itself in fluttering down the many-tracked possibilities of an outlook whose center is amorphous.

—I wonder what his central core actually is—or if he himself knows what it is—or if Mrs. Roosevelt knows—or if he really has one. He seems like a man who wants to dive into the blue waters of the future, but doubts they will bear him up. So instead of diving in he dabbles one foot in a wave while keeping the other planted on the shore. I wonder if the beliefs, impulses, instincts, reasonings, hopes radiating from his center work together because they are integrated at their source, or if they tug among themselves because his core lacks integration. Has he, like Churchill, a reference point to which are hinged all his actions and reactions? Certainly he has tendencies . . . the "rise of the common man" idea. But how far does he want it to go? Does he think democracy is a fetish here too? Does he, way down somewhere, want the "common man" well fed, well housed, well clothed under the paternal eye and benevolent patronage of an "uncommon" man like himself? Does he think that's all that's possible in this world, even in these "democratic" United States? Is he essentially still the squire of Hyde Park? Or does he go all the way—does he want all men, counting himself among them, clothed also in dignity as a human right, without either patrons or beneficiaries?

—It's true that at this stage of our development Roosevelt, to accomplish anything, cannot move too far ahead of the American people; he can move only as fast as the traffic will bear. Is his zigzagging, his bobbing and weaving, due chiefly to this practical consideration, or is it due to a lack of inner direction? Is he beneath his double-talk and demagogy wholehearted and single-minded in his belief that humanity should move forward? Does he think it can? Has he a goal he doesn't lose sight of amid the political chicanery involved in staying on top of the heap? A goal against which he tests all his new ideas, in whose behalf he is seeking ways and means? Or does he entertain a series of changing short-term goals one after the other? Are novelty and the spectacular feat his basic reference point? Is he a kind heart, an adroit brain and a shower of sparks? Or is he these things harnessed to a firm and valuable purpose?

—Fascinating to watch. His personality and

mind glitter from innumerable facets. When you're face to face with him he's terrific. Then you begin to wonder. . . . What is he primarily, at bottom? The chances are that history will fumble a long time on that one. . . .

—Eleanor Roosevelt? My guess is she's extremely important—a big part of F.D.R.'s development. Very different from him; essentially, as a person, maybe superior to him—at least her core is more firm. She supplements him. Who knows when her influence began? Probably very early in their association. And it is likely that only the two of them realize how much she had to do with his ability to rise above his handicap after he came down with polio. Her part in the Presidency now is a natural extension of her part as his wife throughout their marriage. If he can be likened to an imposing, full-sailed ship, she's been the guiding, steadying rudder. If only she's able now to keep him on the course. If only her passion for a decent postwar setup can kindle in him a sustained determination not to give in when Churchill and he tangle on questions concerning the future.

—Tonight Stella and I caught a glimpse of a fragment of the Roosevelt-Churchill drama. The climax, the main chance for the leading man, may still be far off. F.D.R. seems to be an actor who just naturally knows all the tricks. He's writing his own lines, or some of them, as he goes along, and he's determined to retain the star role on the world stage. But will he—can he? Tonight he looked like a billion dollars, healthier than Churchill, who is several years older and now his most obvious rival for the principal role.

—F.D.R. has many advantages over Churchill; but how good a bargain driver is he really? Sound as he seems in the upper part of his body, he can't stand up—will he be able to stand up against his rival and friend—or "friend"—spiritually, politically? If so, will the American people back him up not only in the war but after? Or is he, in spite of his extraordinariness, our leader in so representative a sense that our weaknesses with regard to the world problem are also his? Does he appear so extraordinary because he sums us up so thoroughly?

—No doubt much of this has been rolling about in Churchill's brain during his stay at the White House. And the probability is that F.D.R. has an idea what's going on in that big head.

—Churchill is fascinating as the devil. But there are fewer facets to his character; at least fewer showed tonight. He's the personification of Anglo-Saxonism: aloof, sublimely self-confident, impersonally certain that it is right, noble, good, best; that it is the cultural aristocrat of the world, the natural if not inevitable ruler. You can't call it vain or conceited; there isn't the underlying un-

certainty that gives rise to conceit. The essence of
such people is their complete lack of self-doubt as
to the innate superiority of their breed. Utterly
sure of themselves even in extreme crises, they
feel no need for reassurance. Just now Anglo-
Saxonism is in a dreadful spot, its back against the
wall, but in spite of Munich and Dunkerque, it
hasn't occurred to Churchill to doubt that it is the
obdurate Gibraltar of civilization. England loses
the battles but wins the wars. Or gets them won for
her. Unlike Roosevelt, Churchill does not reach
into the future; in fact he calls the postwar world
"that unattractive jungle" and refuses to discuss it
in public. His idealism glories in the past heroics
of imperialist success, and thrives on it. In him the
British heyday has marshaled its remaining
strength. But it's not enough in this emergency. He
needs help. So he's here. So he's working on F.D.R.
"Mr. President"—

—Right now, while all these people in Constitution Hall, many of them elected representatives of the country, are hearing Toscanini's rendi-
tion of "Death and Transfiguration," Churchill is
in the White House taking all the needling F.D.R.
can hand out from the vantage point of our poten-
104 tial contribution to the victory. But the Prime

Minister of Great Britain is keeping his eye on the ball—the continuance of the Empire at whatever cost to whatever else anyone else may have in mind.

—Conquest *versus* Liberation—

—Well, thank God for Churchill through the Battle of Britain, if one-tenth of what has been credited to him in that episode is true . . . but also for the signs that, with many other nations caught in the war, the British people too are undergoing a transfiguration and eventually will turn away from Churchillian concepts and fixations to seek their new level in a new world tending to equalization not only among individuals in privileged lands but among countries and continents. . . . If only we too undergo a transfiguration in the course of the war.—

Before Toscanini turned around on the podium after concluding the program, Mrs. Roosevelt was on her feet. A few seconds later, escorted by ushers at a running walk, we were rushing down the ramp in her wake, rushing doorward across the empty lobby and into the waiting car.

CHAPTER XI

Home Through the Night

"WHERE are you staying?" Mrs. Roosevelt asked Stella and me as we drove off.

"We're taking a train home tonight," I said. "We couldn't get a hotel room."

"Have you Pullman reservations?"

"No, we're only going as far as Philadelphia. Then it's about an hour's drive to our place in New Jersey. We'll be home by five or thereabouts."

"I'm sorry," said Mrs. Roosevelt. "We wanted to ask you to stay overnight, but there just isn't a room in the House. We had to put up several people in the Prime Minister's party. It's too bad you have that trip tonight. Miss Thompson will take you to the station."

The car went very fast through the almost deserted streets.

"Monroe," Mrs. Roosevelt said, "I forget— where are you staying?"

"The Mayflower."

"You won't mind making your way there by yourself. It's been such a long time since I've seen

you. You're not too tired to come in with me for
a little chat, are you?"

"No, I'd like to," said Mr. Robinson.

The car turned into the White House grounds.

"Thank you again for coming," said Mrs. Roosevelt, shaking hands with us. "Good night."

"Thank *you*, Mrs. Roosevelt. Good night."

The footman motioned me into the seat beside
Miss Thompson.

"Well, it's been quite an evening," I said as we
drove out the Pennsylvania Avenue gate again.

Miss Thompson smiled.

"The President was in great form," I said.

Miss Thompson nodded, then said: "Too bad
you have to go home so late. When Mr. Robinson
called this morning and told Mrs. Roosevelt what
a time he'd had getting a room, she asked me to see
if there wasn't some way of putting you up in the
House if it turned out that you didn't have anywhere else to stay, but there isn't even an extra
bed."

"Mrs. Roosevelt is pretty grand," remarked
Stella.

After a moment's thought Miss Thompson
answered: "I've been with her twenty-odd years
now and all I can say is, there's no one like her."

"The press has been ribbing her plenty of late,"
I said.

"People who criticize her," said Miss Thompson in her even, casual voice, "simply don't know what they're talking about. They don't understand the meaning of her activities. Or they just unconsciously resent her being so different from other Presidents' wives. Or they insist on looking at her from their special political viewpoint. Westbrook Pegler, for instance. But the less said about him the better." She smiled. "Mrs. Roosevelt takes him in her stride, but I can't stand him and his stuff—and I think not only because I'm Mrs. Roosevelt's secretary."

I said it was too bad Pegler had stopped writing about sports.

Pause.

"You won't be getting much sleep tonight either, Miss Thompson," Stella said, "—coming to the station with us."

"Oh this is practically on my way home."

"You don't live at the White House?" I asked.

"No. I used to, but it was a little too much for me. Mrs. Roosevelt understood and I got an apartment outside." Then after a moment: "But this evening I was especially glad to stay, not only on account of the concert. I was curious to see how Mr. Churchill would react to you."

We laughed.

In a few minutes we reached the Union Depot and said good night.

Stella and I changed back to day clothes in the
station washrooms.

It was quarter to twelve. The huge depot was
jammed. Trains were late arriving and leaving.
The New York-bound "milk train" was scheduled
to depart shortly after midnight and we thought
we'd take it rather than wait for a later express.
But then I learned that a train from St. Louis,
which had just pulled in three hours behind time,
was going to Boston *via* Philadelphia. We got on
and found two seats together on the end bench
facing back in a crowded coach.

Twisted in all sorts of uncomfortable positions,
many of the passengers slept. Others sat with dull
expressions on their faces. A man across the aisle
was reading a pulp magazine.

All the curtains were pulled down, perhaps not
so much because of air-raid precautions as to im-
press upon people that we were in the war.

We were tired, but wide awake; and when the
train's rumbling was not too loud, we discussed
the evening.

I told Stella what I'd been thinking about
during the concert. "What do you think of them?"
I asked. "You took quite a shine to Churchill,
didn't you?"

Stella laughed. "It was quite a show. . . . I think
he's cute—maybe a rascal, but cute. I liked watching him—the way he screws up his face and talks

and delivers his lines. It was exciting, funny. I

guess the quality of everything he or Roosevelt says is blown up by the fact that the one is Prime Minister of Great Britain and the other President of the United States. When they're together the enhancement of their lines is simply terrific. Naturally; there's so much involved. . . . The only one I really like is Mrs. Roosevelt—she's tops."

"What did you think of Roosevelt?"

"I don't know—" Stella hesitated. "I haven't any clear feeling about him. You can put your finger on Churchill and Mrs. Roosevelt, but not on him. He's so . . . I don't know . . . so abstracted. Churchill and Mrs. Roosevelt were in the same room with you, while Roosevelt, although I was right there next to him, was on the stage—removed —up there behind the footlights. There was nothing about him as a man that I could hold onto —only the actor, someone enacting a tremendous role, abstracted into the Presidency. . . . I think he's everything and more than I've imagined but, curiously, also less. You don't get the feeling of flesh and blood that you get with Churchill and Mrs. Roosevelt."

"I don't think Churchill is cute," I disagreed. "Didn't you see his mouth, his eyes? Cute!"

"He is, just the same—superficially at least, if you don't think about him and what he stands for. That's not the point though. He's terribly real as

a man. Terrific. Also terrible, when you do think
what he stands for . . . fighting against Fascism *What a Pan.*
and Nazism and at the same time keeping the lid *These*
on most of the world. . . . It's incongruous, crazy, *Two*
but—"

—Will I be free to write up the evening? Right
away? Hardly, if I want to tell the full story, to
indicate that all isn't sunshine and roses between
Roosevelt and Churchill and say what I actually
feel about their relationship as it struck me. There
is a war to win, and I may be accused of trying to
stir up anti-British feeling, to undermine Anglo-
American unity.

—On the other hand, Roosevelt may welcome a
piece about the evening, especially if I suggest
that he's not letting Churchill get away with things.
Such an article may lessen the suspicion current
here and there in the country that he and "Winnie" are too good friends. But why should I serve
such a purpose? I'm suspicious of the relationship
myself. . . . Besides, whatever I may now write
about tonight will have to go through censorship.

—Also, what are the ethics in the situation? Can
a writer dine at the White House, then use the
occasion as material during the President's en-
cumbency? . . .

—Is Roosevelt really interested in *Two-Way
Passage*? Does he mean to encourage me to go on

plugging the idea? To exploit his remarks to Stella and the fact that he made Churchill read the book? . . .

—I'll have to wait and see what happens. Meantime the thing to do is to make the fullest possible notes on the evening.

Driving home from North Philadelphia on Broad Street at five o'clock, we stopped for a bite at a Toddle House, one of a chain of diners. Two or three workmen and a policeman were breakfasting at the counter. The chef-and-waiter had the radio on. Someone was broadcasting "this morning's headlines":

. . . The President appointed Donald Nelson chief of all war production. . . . News from the Pacific continues bad. But the Russians are extending their counterattacks. The Germans have been pushed back south of Moscow. There is tough fighting also in the Crimea. Military experts now think Hitler has overplayed his hand and will have to write off his winter campaign as a dead loss. . . . Wendell Willkie was at the White House yesterday. The President asked him to take the chairmanship of the war labor relations board, but it is believed that Willkie declined—

"I guess that's why Roosevelt didn't mention Willkie," said Stella.

"Perhaps more important," I said, "is that he didn't mention Russia—whatever the reason. He and Churchill must have had all this information last night."

Rising and paying his check, one of the workmen let out a healthy belch.

We got our waffles and coffee.

"Well," said Stella, "from White House to Toddle House."

What a Pair,
These
Two

PART III

AFTERTHOUGHTS: 1942-45

Aside to the Reader: No member of the Roosevelt family and no one present at the dinner saw any part of this book in script.

Parts I and II are based on very detailed notes written immediately after the dinner. The self-quotations in the following two chapters are from my letter to Mrs. Roosevelt (mentioned on page 140) and from diary entries during 1942-1945.

L. A.

CHAPTER XII

Captive of Circumstances

IN A ringing voice on December 9, 1941, F. D. R.
said in Congress and to all the world:

"The true goal we seek is far above and beyond
the ugly field of battle. When we resort to force,
as now we must, we are determined that the force
shall be directed toward ultimate good as well as
immediate evil. We Americans are not destroyers
—we are builders. . . . We are going to win the
war and we are going to win the peace that
follows."

I reread the speech five weeks later.

—The propaganda machine now being set up, I
thought, will weld us into a terrific effort and our
side will probably win the war hands down. F.D.R.
gave a few hints, at least in terms of arms production, how we'll do it. But "the peace that follows"?
He didn't say how we'll win *that*.

—Now we're operating on a mixture of fear,
humiliation and anger that the Japanese struck
into us. F. D. R. is exploiting that to make us do
our stuff in the war. "To win the peace," will he
try to reach something else within us?

—A few years ago he said we had "a rendezvous with destiny." Does he understand the nature of that destiny? What steps will he take to bring us to the rendezvous? . . .

A sentence in an article, "Reconstruction Begins *Now*—Or, How We Can Avoid What We Are Likely To Get," by Lewis A. Dexter, in the February 1942 *Common Sense* magazine hit the nail on the head: "Unless our plans meet the sentiment and desires of the actual living men of the postwar epoch, they have as much chance of being effectively adopted as a meat roast in a nunnery on a Friday in Lent."

I marked two paragraphs in Harold L. Ickes' piece in the *Free World* magazine for the same month:

"In common with all men of democratic aspirations everywhere in the world, I say: Enough! Let us crush the totalitarian infamy once and for all. Let us have peace for ourselves and security for our children by establishing democratic governments everywhere. . . .

"This is the only foreign policy that is worthy of a democratic government. In fact, I am convinced that this is the only kind of foreign policy that will work."

—Is that F.D.R.'s idea too? Is Harold Ickes

trial-ballooning for him? Has Roosevelt bumped into the stubborn conservatism of Cordell Hull and the musty bureaucratic orthodoxy of the State Department? . . .

—Hitler and the forces and circumstances that brought him to power can be really beaten only by a military effort in conjunction with a revolutionary idea which is both sound and more powerful in its appeal than his. I think it will have to be the idea of a *democratic revolution*. Without it Hitler and his Nazis are apt to win even if they're militarily destroyed some years hence. The fire he's started is so big, and its fuel so potent and widespread, that it can be extinguished only by starting another fire.

—To do any good, the idea for a democratic revolution must appear, seize our minds, ignite our idealism, and be put into operation now—as soon as we can pull ourselves together. Such a thing could conceivably happen only in the United States. . . . *Can* it even here? Perhaps not. . . . But only we have the developed, movable material resources. Can we dredge up enough sincerity to convince the European peoples that we mean them well? They'd be inclined to trust us. Owing to our peculiar political history, only we can open the Middle Road to the future which most of the world's peoples prefer to the extreme Right and Left roads when they have an opportunity to choose.

When Julian Huxley arrived in New York early in December 1941 he said: "The United States will be the most powerful country in the world when the war is over, while Europe will be a complete mess."

—When he said "Europe," did he include Britain? The war is impoverishing her. Also, no matter what Churchill may be thinking, her hold on the Empire is bound at least to loosen. . . .

In a letter to the New York *Times* (January 18, 1942) Harold Laski suggested that Britain would have to "adapt" herself and "consent" to all kinds of revolutionary changes or else "even our victory will be no more than the prelude to a long epoch of chaos and confusion, in which much of its possible fruits will be thrown away. . . . The United States, if I may say so, has a quite special contribution to make. Born as a refuge from oppression, united by a war for freedom, accustomed from its outset to affirm the rights of man, it has the experience, not less than the obligation, to lead mankind into the new epoch. The process will be long, for men are not easily habituated to a freedom they have rarely experienced. But if Americans are prepared to be as patient as they have been generous, they have it in their power to make men see what it is that has made Washington and Jefferson, Woodrow Wilson and Franklin Roosevelt a part of the central flame which burns at the heart of the world."

—There's a Britain other than Churchill's. F.D.R. can appeal to this other Britain if he will —*if* he and Churchill haven't already become too great pals. Or if there aren't some other, some overpowering, considerations—if Roosevelt's thinking isn't trapped in our traditional foreign policy, or lack of it . . . in our isolationism which for decades has rested in part on the British Navy, on our playing along with Britain, and her playing along with us, when it came to anything crucial.

—He may be thinking about our being caught between Europe and Asia. Also about the fact that affairs in the Western Hemisphere are pretty chaotic, that his Good Neighbor policy is mostly a phrase, that the Monroe Doctrine isn't what it used to be, and that some of the Latin American countries are anybody's game.

—We're apt to muff things. Beneath all that breezy aplomb of his, F.D.R. is worried. From where he sits right now, our form of government is the most difficult in the world; and as a people, we're just about the most difficult people to do something with that isn't "practical" at first glance or doesn't fit in with our current fetishes. He can't forget Wilson's experience in 1919-1920. His mind must be crisscrossed with uncertainties, and he may be reaching out for anyone . . . anything . . . that seems more or less stable or firm.

—He's a progressive, but a "liberal," a gradualist, and he may have a conscious or unconscious tendency—in spite of his anti-imperialist views—to lean on a fellow like Churchill and even on his Empire because he's afraid of the Leftist outburst in Europe and Asia after the war and wants to forestall it if at all possible.

In his essay "The Young American" Emerson wrote: "I call upon you, young man, to obey your heart and be the nobility of this land. In every age of the world there has been a leading nation, one of a more generous sentiment, whose eminent citizens were willing to stand for the interests of general justice and humanity, at the risk of being called, by the men of the moment, chimerical and fantastic. Which should be that nation but these States?"

—With all of F.D.R.'s imagination, avidity for ideas, flair for vivid leadership, is he capable of feeling, making his own, what Emerson meant? How many other Americans are? Can such a thing be translated into political action? . . .

The December 1941 issue of the *American German Review*, organ of the Carl Schurz Memorial Foundation, carried an editorial:

"One of the most discouraging factors in our life today is the lack of aggressiveness on the part of men of good will. It seems that the forces of evil do not hesitate to carry on in an aggressive way at all times, while those who have a message that would really change the old world too often take on a defensive attitude or envelop themselves in a cloud of inertia and silently pray for better days.

". . . America, during the past three hundred years, has . . . assimilated millions of the oppressed from all over the world. Here we have established liberty and the elements of true democracy, free from the binding traditions of the Old World that have resulted in death for millions of people. We have demonstrated that men of all races, all creeds . . . can live together in peace and fellowship, and serve the best interests of all.

"What is the next step? No one can claim that we have reached perfection, but . . . we have demonstrated the possibilities for the creating of a sane world. Shall we now . . . recognize that unless we can permeate the rest of the world with the spirit of freedom and democracy that we have found in America, it will be impossible for us to survive? A number of people are thinking along these lines . . . that unless the people of the United *Dinner* States can export the ideas of tolerance and good *at the* will, it is only a question of time until we become *White House* like the other nations. . . ."

In mid-January 1942, despite the most fervent wishful thinking among the fear-ridden anti-Russianists and anti-Communists in the United States and Britain, it suddenly became clear that Russia would most probably not fold up, as had been expected since the previous June, but would withstand the Nazi onslaught.

—And if that happens and she becomes a major factor in winning the war, Russia is going to be a great power. How will that affect Roosevelt and Churchill together and separately? And, through them, the postwar world?

—Will it be Churchill's Either-Or?

—Can it be Roosevelt's Middle Road?

—What's Stalin thinking?

—In the drama now shaping up F.D.R. is the key figure. Does he see that only we—and we only if we're careful—can bring about the ideological compromise necessary in the postwar international picture if a sharp cleavage between the West and the Soviet is to be avoided, if chaos and another war are to be prevented? Can he show Britain and *124* Russia that in all probability both will be unable

to guide—and implement—any substantial imme-
diate reconstruction in Europe? That it'll take re- sources only we have or will be in a position to
buy from countries like Brazil, Argentina and
Canada?

On December 14, 1941, Vera Micheles Dean of
the Foreign Policy Association broadcast from
New York:

"As the Russians press on behind the Nazis,
some people in the Western World have begun to
wonder whether victory in Europe may after all
be won by Russia rather than by Britain and the
United States. . . . The Soviet leaders have been
more deft than either British or American statesmen in preparing the ground for a collapse within
Germany. . . .

"It would certainly be grossly exaggerated to
say, at this moment, that any large number of
Europeans would be willing to accept the Soviet
system, even in profoundly modified form, if they
could find some other alternative to the Nazi new
order. Only if the Western powers should fail to
provide such an alternative would the Soviet program have any chance of success. . . . But we must
also remember that the majority of people in
Europe have been profoundly disillusioned during
the past twenty years by Britain's policy toward the   *125*

Continent. If an alternative to both Nazism and Sovietism is to be presented to Europe, that alternative will have to be formulated by the United States, which is regarded by Europeans as the champion of a new and forward-looking democracy. . . ."

—But *can* we provide that alternative? Have we as a people the necessary character, the necessary leadership for such a function? Can we agree on its purpose? . . . The Middle Road? The trouble is that reaction, often very powerful, always resourceful, usually compact and specific of purpose, is out to block and obstruct that road, especially its Left shoulder. Can Roosevelt maintain a strong enough crew during and after the war to keep it clear of obstruction? For, of course, we can't be progressive abroad if we're not progressive at home. . . . And again: Is Roosevelt really committed to progressivism? He tends to want to be all things to all men. . . . Will Churchill find it easy to exploit Russia's rise as a power and seduce him into a counter-revolutionary foreign policy? . . .

Russia?

In World War I, Russian soldiers deserted wholesale. They became a mass base of the anti-czarist upheaval. In this war the soldiers of the Red Army are fighting like mad, dying by the millions, deter-

mined to save their country, their chance for a
better future.

—Here in America one may think ill of the
Moscow Trials and the Russo-German Pact. But to
a great number of the people in the USSR the
revolution of 1917 and the succeeding Five-Year
Plans have been progressive developments. The revolution took power away from the aristocracy,
the priests, the merchants, who under the czars
almost always used it to benefit only themselves,
and placed that power in representatives of the pro-
ducers. Those representatives have been using it
almost without exception to prepare the country
against attack and to benefit—eventually—an infinitely larger number and wider range of people.
Like the American Revolution, the Soviet upheaval was and is primarily anti-imperialist. It kept
Russia's land and resources for her own peoples
and was prepared to defend them when and if
the attack came. It came.

—Now the USSR is linked with us and Britain
in common cause. She's fighting under her tough,
purposeful leaders who have tolerated no monkey
business from anybody inside their borders, however disturbing that's been at times to some of us
living in this relatively favored country.

—Aren't we perhaps too favored? Many Americans are too privileged in their personal lives to

understand Russia which for twenty-odd years has

lived consciously behind a cordon sanitaire, in a state of impending siege. There's a lot of anti-Russian talk here, even now [1942].

—Americans have forgotten that for a while after the Revolution the United States too was under siege. Americans were considered upstarts. In 1812 they had to fight a war to defend the country's independence. When the Civil War came on, official Britain, hoping to make the split permanent, helped the South, while much of the public sentiment in Britain favored the Union cause. Russia aided the North.

—We've grown smug. We tend to look askance at those who differ from us, who may be industrially backward. We are inclined to exaggerate our virtues, overlook our faults. In this I suppose we're like other peoples. Maybe way down we're insecure and we comfort ourselves by emphasizing our accomplishments in order to avoid facing our imperfections. And we don't like to be disturbed. Nobody does.

—Our isolation, our comparative security from direct attack has made us unresponsive to history. Our lack of imagination as to what can happen to us in consequence of events elsewhere and in conjunction with our domestic problems amounts to a
danger.

—How many of us bother to imagine the plight and mood of European peoples after the war?

—When the war is over, are we going to do exactly what I figure Winston Churchill expects us to do?

—Here's where F.D.R.'s leadership will meet its hardest test. Are his own personality and character too tangled up in the now dominant aspects of our national character to be able to rise above them and inspire us to work with the revolutionary democratic, anti-imperialist dynamism which started this country, and to project it to the European lands with which we have, through our new-immigrant groups, so deep a human relationship? Or is he but a vivid shadow—a movie director's idea of how the President of the United States ought to look and act? If so, he hasn't—we haven't—a chance to withstand Churchill's clear, tough imperial purpose and disprove his Either-Or thesis for the postwar era. If so, there's no chance for a Middle Road—eventually none even for ourselves internally. The orthodox Marxists will be proved right—that it's class against class: capitalism *versus* socialism, imperialism *versus* world revolution. We'll be compelled to fight things out on a Right-and-Left basis, here and abroad.

—Limited as he is by being a Tory, Churchill is *Dinner* enormously clever. He's going to exploit our *at the* mutual "Anglo-Saxonism," for all it's worth. And *White House* the fact that we do have the same language and other things in common with Britain is important. But we have things in common with the Soviet Union too.

—F.D.R. recognized the Soviet Union after the Wilson, Harding, Coolidge and Hoover administrations had refused to do so. Did he see the USSR as a forward-moving force in the world, the source of a new dynamism toward general welfare? Does he see that in their beginnings the USA and the USSR have something crucial in common: we're both anti-imperialist?

—Is there anyone close to F.D.R. who knows something of the Marxist way of thinking and is trying to figure out what Stalin and the men around him may be thinking about the postwar period? Not that Marxism is the only thing that shapes their thoughts. But if Roosevelt isn't up on it himself from the American angle, as Churchill no doubt is from the British imperial angle, he'd better have someone close to him who is. . . . Marxism is a partial basis of Russian developments, and he'd do well to keep it in mind as he seems to be aware of, say, the anti-British senti-

130 ment in this country. For a President of the United

States in the 1940's not to know something of Marxist theory and habits of thought is like Sears Roebuck not knowing something of Montgomery Ward's setup and promotion ideas.

—Most of the anti-British sentiment in this country annoys me. I'm opposed to that part of British thinking and acting which tries to maintain its empire system intact without regard for the wishes of many Britishers and of other nations and peoples unfavorably affected by the process of maintaining the Empire. I'm opposed to Tory imperialism in Britain as I am to Tory imperialism elsewhere. In the long run it profits very few, and those but temporarily. It has the British people in a trap. It gets them into wars which, besides killing off the best men, wipe out whatever profit the average Britisher and Britain in general may have derived from the system. . . . It's very questionable if the laboring masses ever derived any benefit from the imperial system. At its height, British cities contained horrible slums. For decades the level of physical health and strength has been extremely low. . . .

—Up to Dunkerque, Britain was the dominant factor on the international scene. It's been said that that dominance, acquired and maintained through balance-of-power, gave the world a longer span of peace than it might have had otherwise. This *Pax Britannica* business hasn't a leg to stand on. In the nineteenth century, a British century, Britain fought—directly or indirectly—more than a score of wars totaling fifty-odd years. Some of them were major conflicts, others operations against African and Asiatic peoples. Then came the Balkan wars, World War I, etcetera, whose causes were intimately involved with British imperialism. . . . Certainly this propaganda about the British Empire being an instrument for peace has no relevance to the present and the future.

—The pressure for freedom, equality, general welfare is growing insistent both in imperial colonies and in countries like Greece and Yugoslavia which used to be nominally independent. Many peoples are outgrowing their political swaddling clothes; now they want to stand upright and walk on their own two feet. When they do stand up—and lots of them are going to try to after the war—they may not walk with as much grace and poise as those who stroll through the world's Foreign Offices, but it will be walking, not crawling.

—Britain won't, can't help them rise and walk; certainly not Churchill's Britain. If we aren't ready to help the now backward countries when the moment arrives, it'll be tragic. The clock won't wait just because we're not ready.

—The governments-in-exile?

—The misery in Europe and the feeling be- tween occupation forces and local populations *Afterthoughts:*
amount to a revolutionary situation which will *1942-45*
come to a head when the Nazi-Fascist power breaks.
The old ruling groups in occupied countries, who
have almost invariably compromised with Hitler
and Mussolini in order to hold onto their interests,
will be swept aside. The people in most of the
governments-in-exile are tied up with these groups,
are personal symbols of spiritual and political
failure in Europe. They're incapable of developing any kinship to a future which is bound to be
revolutionary. They will be pushed aside too.

—Because of their willing or unwilling co-
operation with the Nazis and Fascists, the old
Rightist parties and privileged classes in Europe
are on the chute. We Americans should not try to
sand the chute; let them slide. The best part of our
tradition puts us on the side of the Europeans who
wanted to make Wilson their guide in 1918-1919.
If we follow that tradition, we should get in line
with the historically logical world revolution now
going on. If we are to save the best phases of the
American Way, we should give this revolution
leadership, make it a *democratic* world revolution.
If we can get hold of ourselves as the great international power we potentially are, and if we give *133*

such a revolution a chance to come off in Europe,
we'll inspire democratic forces on other continents
and enhance our own democracy here. Otherwise—

—But who are "we Americans"? Who makes
policy? Our representatives? But *are* they "our"
representatives? Don't most of them represent
mainly the controllers of resources and production? Is F.D.R. basically also that kind of representative? Or is he—or can he become—an exception? . . . The world revolution now going on will
follow, in one way or another, the lines of its own
necessity. Will he go along with it or will his own
class and personal character and our traditional
isolationism lead him to fall into Churchill's re-
actionary-imperialist trap?* . . .

—F.D.R. said Two-Way Passage opens vistas. . . .
But of course his idea-basket contains other items
—tossed into it about one a minute by all sorts of
people. And the Presidential idea-basket is right

* Writing in the June 1946 *Digest and Review*, J. Raymond
Walsh, economist, writer and news analyst, relates that one evening late in December 1941 F.D.R. invited to the White House
a group of columnists and radio commentators to meet Churchill.
"It was a fascinating affair. The talk was good. It ranged up and
down history. . . . [Churchill] was in fine fettle. It was difficult
to resist his charm and eloquence. One feature of the evening
left an indelible impression on me. Churchill again and again
baited the President for his 'foolish concern' about such things
as the TVA, farm security, and medical aid for everyone. . . .
It was half humorous, half serious."

next to the Presidential wastebasket. Its contents change continually. Perhaps nothing stays in it permanently.

—My suggestion has only just dropped in. The other evening it happened to come in handy as a way to needle Churchill before he went home. . . . Maybe F.D.R. decided we'd all dine together on a sudden hunch only that afternoon, perhaps barely in time to notify the kitchen and invite the English girls at the last minute. . . .

—That evening was in the early days of our fighting participation in World War II. I was at the White House an hour and a half. All told I talked with him fifteen minutes at the most. Men like Harry Hopkins, Admiral Leahy, General Marshall, Frank Knox, Henry Stimson, Jim Farley, Jimmy Byrnes, Cordell Hull, Sumner Welles, Adolph Berle, Senators Barkley, Connally and George—some wielders of political power, others possessing abilities he needs—are with him much of the time during hours when decisions are made and procedures determined. Like a horse in harness, each wears his blinders and plods under the whip of problems which he feels duty-bound to push in front of the President at every opportunity. Each has a basket of solutions, inklings, suggestions and plans for policy and legislation and for compromises pleasing or placating some Senator

135

or faction in the Democratic or Republican party *Dinner* or some lobby looking after special interests; and *at the* each wants to empty his basket into the Presi- *White House* dent's.

—The contents of their baskets are conditioned by their concepts of patriotism and national interest, which hinge on their family, class, religious and ethnic backgrounds; by the ups and downs of their business, political or official careers; by what the press and radio are saying about them; by the relationships among themselves and with the President; by their personal and political loyalties outside the government; by the scope of their egos and ambitions, the range of their emotions, the extent and quality of their intellects; by what they ate last night and whether their wives nagged them this morning.

—Almost of necessity at this stage of our political, soc· ., economic and ethnic process, these off·.ials are functionally Emerson's "men of the moment." And they're awfully busy; papers stream over their desks in torrents. They can't help but reject as "chimerical and fantastic" ideas that are incompatible with or that transcend the contents of their baskets or that seem to complicate the day-to-day disposal of their piles of papers. They dance to emergencies. To do that with any sort of grace *136* they cannot welcome anything that might disrupt the established routines of their departments. These routines are based on the accumulation of past experiences—whether the experiences and the resultant procedures are still valid or not, is a question the majority prefer not to see raised. That's the nature of bureaucracy in this country and perhaps nothing can be done about it.

—Roosevelt is different. He has imagination and as top man he can indulge it, at least over his dinner table. Sometimes he lets himself go even in a public address or some political action like Lend-Lease. But not often. He can't very well. If the title "great man" applies to him, it does so chiefly by comparison with other men in the country. In his day-to-day doings he too is a "man of the moment." Almost inevitably. He'd have to be a prodigiously great man to be anything else.

—In a free-for-all democracy like ours, which hasn't yet attained economic, social and ethnic equality and where groups and individuals tumble over one another in pursuit of their self-interest, he's inhibited by all sorts of considerations. When his flair for the exciting and colorful gets the better of him and he tends to forget them, the lesser "men of the moment" remind him. They bring up pending problems whose "practical solutions" insist that he deal with "reality," with "things as they are." When he springs a "chimerical" idea upon them, or tries to shove it down their throats, they reject it. If he insists, they knock its edges off and squeeze the juice out of it. And in most instances he's got to let it go at that. He's got to work at close range with his top officials.

—When you get down to brass tacks—right now, in 1942, to the question of his relationship with Churchill and what he should do toward winning the peace—you strike a dismal, pathetic fact.

—Even this extraordinary man is a captive of outward circumstances which mesh into his own nature. He's hamstrung by mediocre men and by men made functionally mediocre by their positions, by men under the spell of Churchill's dramatic career, by men bent on playing safe moment-to-moment, by men whom the whole system of our society has turned into seismographs registering the force of the people's conflicts—registering mostly the conflicts of those among the people who are sufficiently organized in groups to speak up loudly enough to be heard; and charting what they register in terms of their own immediate self-interest, such as votes, appointments, professional advancement.

—Thus, ultimately, he's hamstrung by the people—or, rather, by the seismograph reports he's handed of the economic, social, ethnic, political tremors within them.

—The best in the American people—their very considerable good will, their pretty strong inclination on some levels to do the right thing—doesn't easily register in most of the political seismographs closest to Roosevelt. The best in this country is too vague, unfocused, unprecise, unorganized, too much in conflict with prevailing notions of self-interest and national interest, some long out of date. It gets indicated occasionally only on such seismographs as Harold Ickes, Henry Wallace, Eleanor Roosevelt.

—Hopeless? Only if the best in the country continues to flounder pointlessly.

CHAPTER XIII

Toward Either-Or

WITH no high expectations but a good deal of curiosity, I sent Mrs. Roosevelt a long letter—a post-Pearl Harbor restatement of my suggestion in *Two-Way Passage.** She promptly acknowledged receiving it and wrote she was giving it to the President.

Five months later I learned that extracts of the letter had been circulated among the top-flight people in the Administration and that most of them were either indifferent or opposed. It seemed that the State and War Departments especially had no use for the essence of the Passage Back suggestion, but some of the men saw possibilities in a few of its minor aspects.

On January 27 and 28, 1942, the press and radio reported voluminously that the first American soldier to land in Europe during World War II —in North Ireland—was a lad named Milton Henke from Minnesota whose parents had immigrated from Germany. It was clearly not by accident that Private Henke was the first off the boat.

* See pp. 243-247.

He was interviewed and questioned about his German background, and his story was broadcast to Germany. Afterward I found out this was done by direction of the Commander-in-Chief.

A week later it was widely reported that the American soldiers in North Ireland who were of South-Irish parentage were asking how soon they could visit their parents' native towns in Eire. Was F.D.R. behind that too, trying to work on De Valera?

This sort of thing kept popping up right along in the activities of the Office of War Information and the Army's Psychological Warfare Section. Most outfits of our invading army in Italy usually had one or two men whose parents had come from the locality which was the operational objective of the outfit. When the objective was reached, these men inquired for their uncles and aunts and nephews and nieces, creating the best possible atmosphere between our forces and the liberated community.

Toward the end of 1942 when the idea for military governments in liberated countries had come up, *Two-Way Passage* was required reading among those formulating the training program for officers in that branch of the service. But little if anything was retained of the gist of the idea.

Yet some of the American military-government

officers did their utmost to carry the best of the American democratic experience to the old countries. One was an American-born son of Italian immigrants. A civil service clerk in the New York City Department of Sanitation, he joined the National Guard in 1936. Five years later when his outfit was activated, he held a captaincy. Soon he was a major attached to General George S. Patton's staff. He took part in the invasion of Sicily and was the ranking AMG officer assigned to the town of Licata. There a novelist-war correspondent ran across him, and he became the Major Joppolo of John Hersey's novel, *A Bell for Adano* (1944), later made into a play and a movie.

Adano (Licata) had Fascist and also pre-Fascist hangovers; and one day a local official muscled into the head of a breadline in which people had been standing for hours. Major Joppolo had to do something about it; he made a little speech:

I want you to be my friends. As my friends, I will consider it my duty to tell you everything I think, for we do not want Adano to be a town of mystery and suspicion.

Adano has been a Fascist town. That is natural, because the country was Fascist, therefore the town was also. But now that the Americans have come, we are going to run the town as a democracy.

Democracy is . . . that the men of the government

are no longer the masters of the people. They are the servants of the people. . . . Who pays the men in the government? The people do, for they pay the taxes out of which you are paid.

Therefore you are now the servants of the people of Adano. I too am their servant. When I go to buy my bread, I shall take my place at the end of the line, and I will wait my turn. You too must behave now as servants, not as masters . . . of the people of Adano. And watch: this thing will make you happier than you have ever been in your lives.

Early in 1942 I used to meet with four friends in New York—George Skouras, an American born in Greece, one of the Skouras brothers prominent in the motion-picture world and Greek War Relief; Nick Cladakis, a young Floridian of Greek parentage, a protégé of Henry Wallace, who had broken up a large milk racket in the Chicago area and now was the administrator of the far-flung milk business in New York State; Joseph Lilly, the well-known journalist, then a member of Mayor LaGuardia's administration; and Nicholas Mirkovich, a young Serb who had recently completed his studies in political economy at the University of California. The five of us groped about for some way to help the United States take a progressive, democratic, constructive part in international af-

fairs. By and by we hit on an idea and I was elected
to write the President, suggesting

that the United States create . . . an American Foreign Legion—it could be called the American Legion
of Freedom—with bases in the Middle East. This
Legion would consist of small and extremely mobile
units of Yugoslav, Greek, anti-Fascist Italian, Bulgarian, Albanian, Jewish and other nationals not now
functioning as fighters in the military war, and would
be under the Stars and Stripes, commanded by American field officers.

Such a Legion could be recruited in part here, in
part in Africa or the Middle East, and in part from
among men who, on hearing of it, would surely escape
from Yugoslavia, Greece, Italy, Bulgaria, Albania and
other countries with the purpose of joining it. . . .

Such a Legion would develop Commandos for raids
on the occupied countries, establish contact with anti-
Nazi leaders there, procure intelligence, serve as a factor in psychological warfare, prepare for the eventual
invasion—

F.D.R.'s reply is reproduced on the opposite
page. About the same time it reached me, the press
and radio reported that "plans for a Foreign
Legion of United Nations citizens . . . are nearly
complete." Fiorello LaGuardia, eager to get into
the war, was drawn into the discussion of the
144 "plans" in the War Department.

THE WHITE HOUSE
WASHINGTON
March 3, 1942

My dear Mr. Adamic:

Your letter of February 3 has been very useful
in the studies and discussions which are in progress
concerning eventual methods of military operations
in enemy-occupied countries.

While the projects which might be worked out
would by their nature be unsuitable for discussion
in correspondence, I can assure you that the Government departments and agencies interested in work of
this kind are giving serious examination to many
factors such as those you mention. They are obliged
of course to coordinate their discussions, since
questions regarding foreign enlistments, finance,
selective service classifications, etc., all enter
into the matter, as well as considerations of general war strategy.

The information and suggestions contained in
your interesting letter, concerning Yugoslavia and
Greece in particular, will be most helpful in this
work.

Very sincerely yours,

Franklin D Roosevelt

Mr. Louis Adamic,

Milford, New Jersey.

But nothing much came of the idea. The British

objected. Some of our "men of the moment" didn't like it. They impaled it on the horns of diverse dilemmas. F.D.R. either lost interest or did not want to buck the British objection or cut through the problems surrounding the idea.

A piece of it was adopted by the Office of Strategic Services, the secret "cloak and dagger" outfit whose exploits (many very admirable) were widely publicized in 1945. The OSS began to take in nationals of other countries as well as Americans with backgrounds in the lands in which the organization meant to operate.

Nicholas Mirkovich was one of the unnaturalized immigrants enrolled with the intention of using him in connection with Yugoslavia.

Nick Cladakis became an air force captain and got himself sent to Egypt, where he thought he might be able to do something about Greece. After he reached Egypt, however, he was completely hog-tied. By the end of 1943 F.D.R. had yielded to Churchill's insistence that the British have the say-so in the "Middle East," which for the first time was expanded to include the Balkans; and the British, working through Americans ready to collaborate with them on their terms, stymied such Americans as Nick who were intent on using America's prestige in Greece to further *146* a democratic setup. One day in the spring of '44, feeling utterly frustrated, Nick, in an off-duty period, went along with an air crew assigned to a dangerous mission. The plane was attacked and damaged. Nick was wounded. The other men parachuted. Nick went with the plane as it plunged into the Mediterranean.

Almost simultaneously, on a Partisan-held Yugoslav island in the Adriatic, the other Nick—Mirkovich—was killed by fire from a low-flying enemy reconnaissance plane. He had gone there from Bari, Italy, not on duty (his job was intelligence analysis, not combat), but out of boredom. He too had not been used.

Letters* came to me by the thousands from Americans of all kinds of backgrounds and walks of life —businessmen, skilled workmen, students, service men and women, labor union officials, social workers, nurses, doctors and other professional people. Several were well known; a few were international figures. Gradually these letters and the occasional meetings with their writers, including Wendell Willkie and Harold Stassen, led me to feel that I was in contact with some of the finest products of the American social and political experience and that for every such person who wrote to me there were vast numbers of other such persons in the country, honest, well-meaning, forward-

* See page 247.

looking, intelligent and tough-minded, unorganized but ready to be mustered for work tied to a definite, energetic American foreign policy aimed at a *democratic* peace.

No such policy developed. Eventually some of my correspondents got into UNRRA, many to be so circumscribed in their democratic inclination that they finally got out.

Toward the end of 1942 I reluctantly tumbled to the realization that, barring some miracle I was unable to imagine, America would not—could not —develop a democratic foreign policy. The letters which continued to pour in showed me that plenty of people would have gone all-out for such a policy if . . . and *if* . . . and IF—

We made the Darlan and Peyrouton deals in North Africa, then the deal with Badoglio in Italy, giving him ample time to slaughter many of the Partisan leaders.

We committed ourselves to the Chiang Kai-shek regime which was fighting less the Japanese invaders than the Chinese popular movement that called itself Communist, although its immediate objectives were not as radical as had been those of the American Revolution of 1776.

For reasons basic to the desires and urges governing large numbers of articulate, aggressively minded Americans as we approached the middle of the decisive twentieth century, and which tied in also with F.D.R.'s character and relations with Churchill, the Roosevelt administration had gone too far in the other direction—too far to the Right and away from the ideological Middle Road upon which, in the postwar period, we might travel with the Russians and the British as well as with peoples of smaller countries.

The Congress of the United States went out of business as a forum for discussing issues and ideas. When some member wanted to speak out he was checked by the State and War Departments on the grounds that he might reveal military secrets or adversely affect one of our allies or some negotiation in progress—all quite plausible on the face of it, but encouraging apathy and indifference and smothering any tendency to draw the American people into active debate and toward vital democratic decisions.

An efficient smothering pillow was the most publicized and perhaps the most active Congressional committee—the Red-baiting, repressive Dies Committee on "Un-American" Activities.

In the armed forces the idea was to keep the soldiers, sailors and marines remote from any understanding of war issues, to have them fight the battles in the spirit of the football field. Not until 1945 did the War Department issue an Orienta-

tion Sheet on the nature and aims of fascism which
Dinner got its teeth into the subject, and then the publi-
at the cation evoked such protests from so many mem-
White House bers of Congress and influential figures in industry
and the church that it was practically suppressed.*

As late as the end of summer in 1943 we had
no American intelligence service in the Balkans,
although plans for our joining the British in an invasion of that region had been on tap continually.
We learned only what the British wished Washington to know about the resistance and quisling
movements in Greece and Yugoslavia. The earliest
information about Yugoslavia to be acquired firsthand by the American Army came in the autumn
of that year, when Major Louis Huot, an OSS
officer in Cairo, made his way overland into Partisan-held territory and brought out Major Farrish,
whom he had sent in by parachute a few months
earlier. For this piece of initiative Huot was
severely criticized by Brigadier MacLean, a
friend of Churchill's and chief of British Intelligence in the Balkans, and was expelled from the
Mediterranean theater of war.† One of his superiors in Cairo was a man whose anti-Commu-

* "I never heard of this Orientation Sheet," I was told by an
unusually avid-minded veteran who served three years in the
Army. "In the outfits I was in there were 'orientation and education' classes conducted by men who didn't know much—most
of them didn't know what they were talking about half the
time."

† Colonel Huot told part of his story in his book *Guns for
Tito* (1945).

nism, operating untrammeled in the absence of an American policy, made him—in spite of his inherent American anti-Britishism—a ready tool of British policy, which in the Middle East was openly anti-Soviet, anti-Slavic and anti-small-nation, and opposed to resistance movements not authorized by British agents.

When George Skouras joined the OSS and went to Cairo early in 1944 with the hope of using the magic word "America" to bring unity to Greece, this same man did everything possible to stymie him in that purpose. Finally he told him, "The British don't want the Greeks united." To others he characterized Skouras as a "damned fool." Nonetheless, Skouras was instrumental in achieving a tentative unity in Greece as his heroic native country's liberation drew near—only to be obliged to witness, when it arrived late in '44, the newest "Greek tragedy"—the Right-Left civil war, which ensued the acts of the British general, Scobie, and his diplomatic assistants who were under Churchill's direct orders, and which led the British troops, in the name of law and order, to come to the assistance of the Greek Right.

At the first Quebec conference, in 1943, Roose-

velt and Churchill had initialed an agreement that
when the time arrived, the United States would
send into Greece a liberation force approxi-
mately equal in number and rank to the British
force. Roosevelt—member of a Greek American
fraternal organization, the Ahepa, and conscious
of long-standing American interest in Greece, the
birthplace of the democratic concept—apparently
wanted the United States to join in her restoration
and in assuring her an opportunity to acquire a
democratic government. But this didn't suit
Churchill's book.

Awhile later, according to a firsthand, completely reliable source within the Administration,
Churchill reopened the subject. He told Roosevelt that Greece was a British patch of onions, that
Americans had no business there. When F.D.R.
replied that the American people wanted Greece
to get a decent deal, Churchill said the American
people were not really interested, and he offered
to prove it. "Listen to my next speech," he said.
In that speech he fulsomely praised King George
of Greece and King Peter of Yugoslavia, insisting
it was imperative for the sake of stability and

civilization that both monarchies be restored. A few days later he informed F.D.R. over the trans- atlantic telephone that his Embassy in Washington had reported no appreciable reaction on the part of the American press and people to what he had said on the subject of the Greek and Yugoslav kings. Thereafter Roosevelt left Greece to the British.

During the first half of 1942 I continued to think off and on that if F.D.R.—"his own Secretary of State"—had tried to work out an aggressive, dynamic foreign policy favoring democracy abroad and striving for an ideological compromise, he could have evoked much support in new-immigrant groups as well as in sections of old-line American elements. Then I was obliged to realize that that had been precluded immediately after the Japanese pushed us into the fighting part of the war.

A few days after Pearl Harbor the State Department issued a release composed by Assistant Secretary Adolph A. Berle, which behind its cleverly ambiguous verbiage sharply warned the new-immigrant groups. To preserve the unity of the country in order that we might wage war successfully, they were to refrain from starting movements concerning their old countries such as had troubled the government during World War I. This, naturally,

had a depressing effect.

Mr. Berle got himself an assistant to travel about
the country spotting developments in the "foreign sections." Presently this fellow's function mushroomed into the Foreign Nationalities Branch of the Office of Strategic Services. The branch, employing hundreds of people, was headed by DeWitt C. Poole, "an old State Department man," as he called himself, also, as I gathered from conversations with him, an expert (from the conservative angle) on Russia. Personally charming, with a disarming offhand manner; patriotic in the orthodox sense, he was a good official executing his duties according to the policy laid out by his superiors in the State Department.

In 1943 this OSS branch published a 185-page handbook entitled "Foreign Nationality Groups in the United States." It was stamped CONFIDENTIAL but one saw it on numerous desks in Washington. Prepared under Poole's supervision, the publication emphasized that the new-immigrant groups were *foreign minorities*—that is, not integrated into the standard-American population—and so required special attention. There was a chapter on each of the following elements: Albanian, Arab, Armenian, Austrian, Basque, Belgian, Bulgarian, Carpatho-Russian, Czechoslovak, Danish, Estonian,

Finnish, French, German, Greek, Hungarian,

Italian, Latvian, Lithuanian, Netherlands, Nor-
wegian, Polish, Portuguese, Rumanian, Russian,
Spanish, Swedish, Ukrainian and Yugoslav. The
new-immigrant English, Scottish, Welsh and Irish
were not included, although many of them, as
well as some of their American-born descendants,
were, to my knowledge, at least as alien to what I
considered Americanism and as interested in their
old countries as the most "foreign" in the groups
that were listed. Nothing was said about special
resources within the "foreign minorities" which
might be useful in the war effort or to advance
democracy in the world. The groups were presented as problems amounting to a Problem—
something to be watched.

By and large, Poole's purpose, and that of his
organization, was negative, in line with Berle's: to
treat the new-immigrant groups not as integral
parts of America with unique qualities which
could be used to advantage, but with suspicion as
including potential subversive elements, and
thereby indirectly keep them from developing
positive movements with regard to postwar political setups in Europe. Not that there were no subversive factions among immigrants. But they were
few and small, and were handled (or should have
been) by the F.B.I. without hampering or intimi-
dating or reflecting upon the great loyal majority.

In my view, Poole's organization functioned

with extremely unfortunate results. Clever and subtle, it was perhaps more damaging to the American spirit than were the brutal anti-German hysteria and Palmer persecutions of the foreign-born during and after World War I. The general public who might have objected, as some individuals and groups did to putting Japanese Americans in concentration camps, knew nothing about it.

Behind it all was Adoph Berle's negativism, brilliantly logical within its own frame, narrowly patriotic, essentially isolationist, wittingly or unwittingly falling in with Churchill's postwar anti-Russian, anti-democratic intentions, and furthering the actualization of his Either-Or thesis by contributing to the decline of the American spirit which has become so obvious during 1945-1946. Berle's negativism, I am satisfied, was approved by Cordell Hull; also by Hull's special assistant, Leo Pasvolsky, an anti-Soviet refugee from Russia.

All of it was based on a concept of what America should be and what her interests were that seemed to me more akin to the things we were fighting against abroad than to the principles of freedom, equality, democracy which underlay my idea of what America was and what her interests should
156 be.

As it worked out in Poole's OSS activities, Berle's attitude toward the immigrant groups re- sulted in encouraging movements to sustain or restore monarchical, clero-Fascistic, reactionary setups in Austria, Hungary and Yugoslavia. It favored the Habsburg archdukes, Otto and Ferdinand, then swimming in the stagnant puddles of Washington and New York society; Tibor Eckhardt, an agent of the landowners in Hungary; and Konstantin Fotich, then Yugoslav Minister (later Ambassador) in Washington, and Bishop Dyonisie of the Serbian-Orthodox Church in the United States, who both favored a Greater Serbia rather than the restoration of Yugoslavia. It schemed to bring about an east European cordon sanitaire against the Soviet Union, which left the Soviet Union no choice but to scheme to bring eastern Europe firmly within her own sphere. It helped to set off power politics of the most deplorable variety. Philosophically it was based on Guglielmo Ferrero's "legitimacy" concept, lately discovered by the State Department intellectuals, which supported what wished to be static regardless of how dynamic the world had the bad taste to insist on being.

The Berle purpose was aided by a law sponsored by the State Department and passed by Congress requiring anyone actively interested in the form of government of any foreign country to register with the Department of Justice as a "foreign agent." Hundreds of people, but relatively few of the 26,000 known British agents, were forced to register. Sent the registration forms a number of times, I refused to fill them out, maintaining that I was not an isolationist and that, believing the United States should participate in world affairs, I was logically concerned with governmental forms in other countries; that my interest in European reconstruction was motivated by what I considered the national interest of the United States.

The Dies Committee sent agents to Milford, New Jersey, near where I live, to ask questions and try to make me suspect in the community, whose population of some six hundred is typically American in that the majority had no inkling whatever of the political machinations within the war effort that were aimed at the postwar era; also in that they told me of the snoopers, laughing, wondering what it was all about.

During 1943-1945 three members of the committee denounced me four times in the House, restricting themselves to distortions, half truths, and lies furnished them, in part, by Fotich's researchers. Once, in 1944, the UNRRA was attacked because the director of its training center at the

University of Maryland had invited me to give a couple of talks to his trainees.

For a while my telephone was tapped—by whom exactly I don't know. This was annoying quite apart from its illegality; when they tap your line you can't hear as well. One day I said to a friend who called: "Look, this phone is tapped. But don't let that stop you. Let's talk as freely as we would otherwise. In fact let's go into causes. Maybe whoever is listening in will learn something." Soon after that the line ceased emitting the occasional noises that go with tapping.

Sordid as this whole business was, it had its funny moments.

Such are the ramifications, size, and schizophrenic character of the United States Government, particularly in wartime, that its Right often does not know what its Left is doing, and the other way about. While one section in the Department of Justice was trying to register me as a foreign agent, I was helping with scripts for a morale-building radio show sponsored by the Immigration and Naturalization Service, another section of the Department of Justice, and the Treasury Department was sending me on tours to persuade people to buy war bonds and writing me appreciative letters of thanks. And at the same time that my telephone was tapped and that members of the

Dies Committee were sniping at me from behind their Congressional immunity, bits of the Passage Back idea (minus of course its democratic-revolutionary essence) were being used by the government.

Early in 1943 the press reported that Fiorello La Guardia was to be made a brigadier general and put in charge of an unspecified mission connected with Italy and the Balkans, and that I was to be commissioned as one of his aides. Nothing came of it.

For two or three days one week early in the spring of 1944 I received almost no first-class mail. Then it came in a large pile. I was sure it had been held up by some secret agency interested in my doings, views and contacts. In the pile of letters was one from F.D.R. replying to a communication in which I had urged the abandonment of all plans for a full-scale invasion of the Balkans by the American and British forces, and suggested that, instead, we supply Tito's Partisans with heavy matériel and facilitate the Yugoslavs' self-liberation. In making this suggestion I had had the expert help of some of my American military friends lately expelled from the British-controlled Mediterranean theater of war. Thanking me for it, F.D.R. assured me that everything possible was being done to help the Partisan forces in Yugoslavia. . . . After

reading his letter, and looking at the heap of mail
that almost surely had been examined, I unbuckled
my belt and laughed. . . .

Finally, in the summer of 1944, when the last of
the plans for an Anglo-American invasion of the
Balkans (which Churchill had preferred all along
to an invasion through France)* was being mulled
over by the Allied Chiefs-of-Staff, OSS recruiting
officers inquired if I would join their organization
and go to Yugoslavia as an attaché of the American
commanding general. By then Tito's Partisans
had simultaneously liberated two-thirds of the
country from the Axis forces and from the Chet-
niks of Drazha Mikhailovich. Mikhailovich had
had full Anglo-American support through much
of the war, even after it was known to the State
Department and the Foreign Office and to Roosevelt and Churchill personally, that Chetnik com-
manders responsible to Mikhailovich were collaborating with the Italian and German com-
manders in order to procure arms with which to
fight the Partisans. (American OSS and British
Intelligence analyses of the Yugoslav situation—

* Churchill's political purposes in Allied military strategy are
touched on in two volumes published early in 1946 during the
writing of this book: Ralph Ingersoll's *Top Secret* and Harry C.
Butcher's *My Three Years with Eisenhower*. It is to the credit of
the American High Command—particularly General George
Marshall—that it resisted those purposes; sometimes, I suspect,
without support from the Commander-in-Chief.

dated June and September 1944—both state that
Mikhailovich was collaborating with the enemy.)
But by the time this tentative offer of an OSS job
was made to me I had developed a profound distrust of much of the official Washington which
touched on foreign policy. I did not decline to be
used; but, bearing in mind what had happened to
Cladakis and Mirkovich, and how Skouras was
being pigeonholed in Cairo, I stipulated such conditions* that the idea of giving me the job was
dropped. And nothing came of the Anglo-American invasion of Yugoslavia anyhow. The American Chiefs-of-Staff would not go along with the
British idea for it.

So Winston Churchill, in Italy that summer—
only a few days after his meeting with Tito, during
which tears came to his eyes as he embraced the
Yugoslav Partisan commander—held a series of
secret meetings in Rome with representatives of
the Mikhailovich cause in Yugoslavia, the Horthy
crowd in Hungary, the reactionary parties in Rumania, the Habsburgs in Austria, the anti-Russian
Poles, the semi-quislingist Bulgarians and the
royalist Greeks to determine what might be done
about the "Communist menace" in eastern Europe.
These meetings extended through two weeks while
the Second Front was in full swing. But they were

  * See p. 271.

of the Yugoslav government-in-exile alleged" that
I was one.

The Mikhailovich legend was a hoax perpetrated
by the Yugoslav government-in-exile. The Yugoslav government-in-exile, with the boy-king, were
in London, enjoying the backing and guidance of
the Foreign and War Offices. And official Washington was stringing along with official Britain.

Official Washington, reflecting the uncertainties
splitting many Americans, was paralyzed by its uninformed fear of Russia, the Slavs, Communism. At
bottom, it lacked faith in the American Way, not
believing that American democracy could develop
economically, socially, politically so as to satisfy
a great majority of the American people. A satisfied
people can't be bothered by any other ideology
than that which gives them satisfaction. . . . Under
the psychological stress of fear and absence of
faith, enhanced by the other factors I have mentioned, official Washington acted almost entirely
to bring about Churchill's Either-Or.

This process was assisted by foreign and domestic
agents with varying aims, few of which favored
postwar democracy. One evening when the 1942-
1943 winter uproar about the Second Front was
nearing its height, a newspaperman friend took
me to a party in a Washington hotel suite. Several
prominent persons were there and some I did not

know. Among the latter was the English-born wife of a member of the House of Representatives. The room was noisy when I was introduced to her, and she didn't hear my name. For a while I listened to her hold forth about Russia to a fairly high-ranking Administration official. The Reds were essentially no better than the Nazis; and so on. She got onto the subject of Yugoslavia—Stalin was reaching for the Balkans. I ventured to correct her: the Yugoslav Partisan movement was indigenous—whereupon she said, "You talk like that Communist Louis Adamic." I told her I was no Communist. Nor was the *Saturday Evening Post,* which had lately published an article of mine on the situation in Yugoslavia, a Communistic magazine. I nearly added that people like her—busy all over Washington and other vital centers trying to influence Americans and American policy away from an international ideological compromise—were doing more than anyone else to spread what she called Communism.

—How are the Russians taking this sort of thing, I thought off and on during 1943-1944. They must know about it and they can't possibly regard it philosophically. To them it must look like the same old story: the Western world ganged up against the Soviet Union.

—Suppose a Second Front doesn't materialize for some time? Suppose Churchill is right in claiming

we can't invade Europe from the west, or that
F.D.R. and our chiefs-of-staff yield to him even if
he's wrong?* What can the Soviet leaders do but
assume that the United States is basically anti-
Russian? And if they make that assumption, what
else can they plan as their future procedure but
straight old-fashioned power politics? It's a sure bet
that somewhere in the Kremlin some of the best
Soviet brains are thinking postwar politics, pon-
dering schemes to thwart whatever the "Anglo-
Americans" may have in mind that's unfavorable to
the USSR. . . .

—An unfortunate phrase—"Anglo-Americans."
Who's popularizing it? It crops up everywhere—
press, radio, private talk in Washington hotel
suites. And it's hard to protest against, for of course
England and America are working together. They
should be. The trouble is that the phrase is beginning to have subtle—and not so subtle—anti-
Russian connotations.†

* The behind-the-scenes struggle over the Second Front was
widely gossiped about in Washington and New York. As I look
back to 1942-1945, when I spent much time in Washington,
there seem not to have been very many "secrets" I didn't hear
about, often before it was safe to mention them, although I made
no effort to learn them. Some of the people holding fairly important positions whom I met here and there impressed me as
dilettantes afflicted with an ego-driven necessity to blab about
official matters. They were bursting with secrets, and a couple of
cocktails opened them up.—L. A.

† This "Anglo-American" business reached a climax at the
United Nations Conference in San Francisco. Wrote Frank   *167*

Dinner at the White House Early in 1942 a friend of mine who had just become head of a department within the Office of War Information told me that Donald J. Hall, a British Embassy official, wanted to meet me.

Hall turned out to be a very nice man. He had written a travel book on Rumania and knew a good deal about the Balkans. He asked me to telephone him whenever I came to Washington, and invited me to his house for lunch and dinner. We talked of all sorts of things, including the British

---

Smothers in the June 3, 1945, Chicago *Sun* under the title of "Some Anglo-American Herrenvolk among Us":

"A few days ago a young Briton asked me: 'Aren't you worried too much about backing "democracy" in Europe? I want the well-being of those people. But the only countries anywhere that have made democracy work are yours and mine and the British dominions and maybe Switzerland. (He doubtless would include the Scandinavian lands.) France hasn't made it work and most of Europe hasn't developed it at all. They haven't because they are not suited to democracy, and they'll be happier without it.'

"Such is far from typical of British and American attitudes, but too many people of privilege in both countries [holding key positions—*L. A.*] think in that general trend. . . . In certain Anglo-American circles at San Francisco—including a certain portion of the press, and I do not mean the blatantly anti-Russian press—there has been a comfortable assumption that Anglo-American political morals are normally to be taken for granted, and Russian political morals to be suspected of the worst on every issue. It was counted 'good form' in such circles to drink cocktails in high indignation over the arrest of the 16 Poles, but 'bad form' for Indians like Mrs. Pandit to remind the press of the incarceration of Nehru and thousands of other Indians who desire the emancipation of their country. Similarly, no doubt, some British opposite numbers of Americans who soft-pedal the colonial issue would consider it bad form were a Russian, in discussing human rights, to mention the existence of the poll tax and Jim Crow in America. . . ."

Empire; and he assured me that most Britishers were as anti-empire as I was, but of course the Empire was a fact you couldn't dispose of with a shrug or a bit of profanity. Its problems touched not only Britain and the different parts of the Empire but the world at large, especially the United States.

At times Hall was quite convincing as a liberal much perturbed by what I called the "empire racket"—the phrase at once amused and annoyed him. And I was disposed to make friends with him, but all I could manage were the motions of friendliness, for every now and then I suspected that that was all he was doing.

He was very much interested in the progress of the Two-Way Passage idea, in my impressions of anti-British sentiment in the United States, in what I knew of developments in the enemy-held Balkans; and I could not doubt that he had been assigned to study me. I discovered he knew things about me which only someone with a special purpose would bother to find out.

In 1943 he was quite eager beneath his reserve for me to go to Britain. He would arrange for air transportation, and I would be afforded every opportunity to see everything and to talk with Foreign Office people and others. He hinted that Britain and the United States had a common mission in the world, and he wished me to know what Britain

really was. Two or three times he asked if he
might get me a special invitation, that is, if I
would accept it if it came; and I was tempted to
tell him to go ahead, but didn't. I was reluctant to
be under any obligation to a foreign government.

Toward the end of 1943—shortly before he
returned to England to become secretary to Richard
K. Law, Parliamentary Under Secretary of Foreign
Affairs—I noticed that the phrase "Anglo-American" was cropping up in Donald Hall's conversation.

—What does the Teheran agreement really amount
to? I wondered early in 1944. Are these rumors
true of a scene between Stalin and Churchill? Will
the full truth about this Big Three conference
ever come out? For all our vaunted free press, the
American people don't know what's going on. Too
many are taken in by the external trappings of a
conference in distant exotic Iran. Most Americans
seem to have no interest in what actually happened there. The press and radio aren't coming
to grips with it. F.D.R.'s public report was unsatis-
factory.

—On the surface the agreement appears to approach the idea that the capitalist and Communist
systems can coexist in the world. Is this F.D.R.'s
170 work? Can he effect the Great Compromise? With

Churchill at his elbow? I think that American capitalism (with some changes in structure and in the thought habits of influential people) and Soviet socialism (with some changes in outlook) *could* coexist for a long time, conceivably until they leveled off into a similar way of life containing some of the best aspects of both. Each country needs a better knowledge of the other's pattern of thought and feeling.

—But I doubt if Soviet socialism and British imperialism could coexist peacefully for long. They are too different in character and purpose: mass welfare *versus* exploitation. Geopolitically they impinge on one another too intimately, too aggravatingly at a dozen points. And if they can't coexist, whose side will we take? If that of British imperialism, another war is certain. If that of the USSR, it may not be.

—In spite of my "tendency to utopianism," as T—— [a friend] calls it, the Teheran agreement seems too good to be true. The needed ideological compromise can't be achieved in a secret meeting of three men. This is Caesarism, and it can't work in this day and age. If Roosevelt wants to pull it off he'll have to draw in the public opinion of a large part of the world; and he shows no signs of doing that.

—These rumors about F.D.R.'s frequent phone conversations with Churchill and their extensive correspondence said to have begun in 1939 and to run into over a thousand exchanges of cables, letters and memoranda. One can believe them after seeing the two together. If this correspondence exists,* it must contain political and historical dynamite which Roosevelt cannot desire to see exploded, and that a fatal bond between them, favoring Churchill's purposes. . . . What's Harry Hopkins' role in all this? Bernard Baruch's? . . .

—This rumor of the argument over Hong Kong between F.D.R. and Churchill in Egypt while waiting for Chiang Kai-shek. Maybe Churchill did bang his fist on the table and yell at the President that Hong Kong was Britain's business exclusively. Rumor does not say what Roosevelt did then. Can he bang his fist on the table too? Or does he say No with urbanity?

—The terrific dimensions of our material might now being thrown into the war make Britain a second-rate power; why doesn't F.D.R., if he's serious about the Four Freedoms and the Atlantic Charter, make use of that fact to put Churchill in his place? What keeps him from doing it? His advisers? Considerations of wartime unity? Per-

* In mid-April 1945 Churchill confirmed the existence of this extensive correspondence between him and his "friend," who had died a few days before.

haps; but Britain would have to take it anyhow. Is Roosevelt waiting for the war to end before telling Churchill off? Will he do it then? . . . If he discovers that Soviet socialism and British imperialism are incompatible, will he put us on the side of the British? Has Churchill got him all sewed up?

—War operations always bristle with politics. Ours and Britain's in this war bristle with the sort of politics that don't bode well for postwar peace. Right now, from the bits that pop through the "voluntary censorship" screen, the picture of the international situation can only be entitled "The Irrepressible Conflict," and my guess is that it suits Churchill perfectly. In fact he painted much of it.

—The Marxist thesis about imperialism as part of the world-wide class struggle may turn out to be right. Churchill is bent on proving it right. Roosevelt does nothing to inhibit him.

—Not that it's all our fault for failing to develop a dynamic American foreign policy. Or that Churchill's imperial fixity is the only negative factor. The Russians are difficult to understand for people who are not naturally sympathetic to them. When it comes to what we call public relations, they're nowhere. They either don't know how to present themselves to a people like us or they don't care very much what we think of them.

If it's the latter, it's a serious mistake. It'll make for terrific difficulties. . . . Or maybe they figure that a thing like Stalingrad plus the fact that the Red Army is engaging eighty per cent of the Nazi military power ought to speak for itself to all the world.

—Roosevelt and Churchill [in 1942-1943] officially recognized the glory of Stalingrad and the strategic importance of that victory. Their words echoed through the Allied world. But few Americans have thought out the matter of Russia in the postwar epoch and our relations with her.

—The USSR is "Communistic," "totalitarian," certainly "not democratic in our sense" (why should she be?). Internally Russia is many things that we, in our comparatively privileged situation, object to. . . . But when anti-Russianists are brought to admit that without the Soviet Union we and Britain probably could not win the war (nor could the USSR without us) and when finally they are brought to admit that without some of the features they object to, the Soviet Union would not now be militarily powerful, would not be making her incalculable contribution to our common victory, they still remain anti-Russian on the score that the USSR is Communistic, totalitarian, etcetera. *174* In their minds, Russia is pigeonholed in two isolated compartments: thank God for the wonderful Red Army; beware the menace of Red Communism. They want to eat the cake but at the same time they don't want to touch it. There's no coping with such thinking. It's not thinking. It's fear, a hangover from all the ignorant Red bogey talk since 1918. It's hysteria. Some of it exists spontaneously; most of it is stimulated. And F.D.R. does nothing to stop those who stimulate it, does nothing to ameliorate the dangerous confusion on the subject of the USSR which exists in the American people as a whole. Doesn't he want to? *Could* he do anything? . . .

—He's probably trying to achieve a real, faithful co-operation with the Soviet Union which would carry over into the postwar era. Apart from his too close tie-up with Churchill, the difficulty perhaps is that he's afraid of extreme Leftist developments in Europe and Asia, possibly even in America; that he wants—hopes—to curb Soviet socialism; and that that purpose or hope, which Churchill encourages in him every chance he gets, is a drag on his efforts. . . .

As the war passed from the dark days of 1942 to the brightening military prospects and victories of 1943-1944, F.D.R.'s "fireside chats" and other speeches grew more and more disappointing. *175*

Sometimes he talked to the American people like a father to his adolescent children. Sometimes he led cheers for Bill Jones and Frank Kovacs at the front and on the production line. He evidently did not regard us as capable of grasping the central facts of contemporary life. We had to be cajoled, tricked into unpleasant effort, fed on pap. We couldn't be taxed to pay for the war as we went along. We had to be sold bonds and promised profit on them.

—As a politician, I thought in 1944, perhaps he's right. But as the American leader the situation demands, he's terribly wrong. He ought not to cater to the worst in us. He ought to evoke the good and the tough in our national fiber.

—But to do that he'd have to get into the issues of this crisis. He'd have to show us that World War I and II are not separate events but parts of the same thing—explosive symptoms of the vast episode in history which began considerably before 1914. He'd have to show us that this episode consists of war and revolution, primarily revolution and resistance to it, mostly in the shape of war and threats of war; and that to resolve the situation we Americans will have to think and act greatly; to reorganize our minds, reorganize and unify our country, make it truly democratic, economically, socially, ethnically, politically. *But*—

—I must not forget that we are a split people, a fact F.D.R. must reckon with. Split not only as between group and group, class and class, interest and interest. Split also—and less simply—within our individual selves. It is true that there is in the American people a wealth of the kind of qualities needed for such a democratization, and a great desire to undertake it. It is equally true that there is strong resistance against any such thing.

—As President, F.D.R. finds himself in the middle of this split.

—If he would make an honest, vigorous plunge into the issues of the current crisis, he'd probably have an even chance of getting the support of the majority of the people, including most of the army and navy personnel. But most of his generals and admirals and Cabinet officers, and most of Congress and the "kitchen cabinet" and the outstanding people in industry, business, church and education, and even in labor—people at the controls—would turn against him. And they would be able to confuse much of the majority supporting him.

—He wouldn't take the chance. He can't. He's Franklin Roosevelt of Krum Elbow, Dutchess County. He's no revolutionary, he's a fixer-upper. He's mainly intent on preserving the essence of what is, of what he and people like him are attached to and think that others are or ought to be   *177* attached to too.* And the others more or less are, in good times. . . . And if he did want to take the chance, perhaps he'd upset the military applecart, which he can't do—mustn't risk doing—right now. As it is, to get enough production out of industry to win the military war, he's got to go along with the big boys and allow big profits. He must discard his own New Deal and talk of "Dr. Win-the-War." He's emphasizing his role as Commander-in-Chief in which he's doing all right.

—Unlike much of the world, the United States isn't in the grip of a tight revolutionary situation. In their daily lives many people are well satisfied with things as they are—their only desire is to keep them that way. The war is making some people only more satisfied. Americans live from day to day, year to year, and right now—fantastically enough—many are making better money than ever before. The word "revolution"—even "democracy"—scares such people. We're drowning in prosperity. Since we—or a good many of us—are satisfied at home, with unbombed cities and an unravaged homeland, what is there to impel us to take over the job of furthering democracy elsewhere—let alone here?

* According to Grace G. Tully, F.D.R.'s private secretary for many years, "he reserved his supreme scorn for those who parroted the phrase that 'he is a traitor to his class.' How he laughed at those words!"—From an article in the *New Republic*, April 15, 1946.

—Apart from the relative few whose sons or husbands are being killed or maimed, we're so well off that we're practically in a spiritual coma. And in this state it is impossible for us to demand a democratic foreign policy and help resolve the crisis whose issues Roosevelt so carefully avoids. Wallace and Ickes touch on them—and get nowhere.

—This is one of the most important facts in the world. Another is that, with Stalingrad behind her, the USSR will be a great power.

—When the war is over a huge vacuum will exist in the area between these two facts. The Soviet Union—with her dynamism—will move into the vacuum, is already moving—is being sucked—into parts of it. And we—static—will fear her, hate her.

—All of which will not avert the "Irrepressible Conflict."

In the spring of 1944 there was a rumor that F.D.R. wasn't looking well.* I discussed it with a friend of mine in the Administration who saw him every two or three months. He respected the President very deeply, and I never said anything to

---

* Harry C. Butcher's diary, published in *My Three Years with Eisenhower*, contains this entry: "Friday, April 14, 1944. Ed Stettinius told me the President was far from well and is increasingly difficult to deal with because he changes his mind so often." And a few days later, April 17, there is an entry about General Wedemeyer who remarked to Butcher how badly the President looked.

offend that feeling. Early in the summer he volun-
teered his view that what ailed the President might
not be primarily physical. "What I mean is," he
said, "it may be due at least in part to something in
his mind."

"You mean he's baffled?" I asked.

"Perhaps that's it," said my friend cautiously.
"I noticed something wrong soon after Teheran.
I've heard the rumors about that meeting, but I
don't know what happened there or in Cairo. I do
know that directly afterward a decline set in. You
won't mind if I don't talk about it—perhaps
'baffled' is the word. Of course I don't mean to
suggest there's anything immediate to worry
about."

"He'll run again?" I asked.

"He has no choice. I believe he's absolutely sincere about wanting to go back to Hyde Park. In his
state of mind and health, he'd be insane if he
didn't want to—if only to have a few years for reflection and to annotate his papers. Also I think
Mrs. Roosevelt wants him to get out of the White
House. But he can't afford not to run. He's a prisoner of the situation. If he withdrew now—at
practically the last moment—the period before the
next President took office would approach chaos.
His withdrawal would raise hell at home—in the
Democratic party, full of tensions anyway and

now in a dither over who'll run for Vice President; and in the country at large. And it would have unimaginable repercussions abroad. It would almost certainly prolong the war."

I hesitated a moment, then said, "If by some miracle the Republicans should nominate Willkie, I'll vote for him."

There was a long pause before my friend answered. "I can't guarantee what I'm going to say, but I feel quite certain about it. Strictly between us two, I believe the President would like to see Willkie run against him—and win. Willkie doesn't like him, but I think he likes Willkie. If such a thing were possible in our political setup, he'd want Willkie for his running mate on the Democratic ticket; then in a year or so he'd resign and get into the United Nations. I think that for some time now he's been putting most of his international eggs in that basket."

"The United Nations idea?"

"Yes. I know you're critical of our foreign policy, but the difficulties he faces here and abroad are almost incredible. . . . I'm not apologizing for the Administration. I think that with all his 'warts,' as somebody recently called his faults, the President is a very great man. I think too that if nothing happens to him within the next few years, most of the things you and I now dislike will take a turn for the better. This may be old-fashioned American optimism, but it's how I feel. . . . You've been keeping up with some of the developments very closely, but as yet I don't think any of us has much of a perspective on them."

In one of the five conversations I had with Willkie during 1942-1944, he told me of his engagement to see Churchill at the White House during Churchill's second wartime visit to the United States in June 1942.

"When I got there," said Willkie, "the usher informed me that the President would like to see me for a minute before I went up to the Prime Minister's room. He was his usual lively self, talking a mile a minute but saying nothing specific that justified spending his time and mine, to say nothing of Churchill's, who was waiting for me upstairs.

"Then he said he'd take me up to Churchill. I protested, but he said it was no trouble, he welcomed a break in his work. So he got into the wheelchair and his valet pushed him through all those corridors, into the elevator and out of it, and into Churchill's room, while I walked along."

Willkie seemed to avoid mentioning Roosevelt by name or title whenever possible. It was usually "he."

"In Churchill's room he kidded awhile, saying

nothing much, and after a few minutes remarked, 'Well, I'll leave you two highbinders alone now,' and motioned the valet to take him out.

"But Churchill waved the Negro aside. 'This is my job, my friend,' he said. He stuck the big cigar in his mouth, gripped the wheelchair and pushed it slowly, ceremoniously, out of the room while Roosevelt cocked his cigarette holder, crooked his neck around, and smiled up at him." Then Willkie's husky voice rasped with sharp emphasis: "I was *shocked* by the implication, haunted by the phrase 'taking him for a ride,' which came to my mind.

"When Churchill had the chair in the corridor he turned it over to the valet. Then he came back and closed the door. I looked at him as hard as I could, trying to show him I saw through his game. Churchill got it, and his whole face and the top of his head turned beet red.

"He looked abashed, pathetic, almost pitiable for a minute. After all, the guy is Prime Minister of Great Britain and one of the great war leaders of all time. He fumbled with his cigar, and all of a sudden he seemed a dumpy little man. Do you know what I mean?"

I nodded.

"Then he got hold of himself. By sheer will power he threw off his embarrassment. His color receded and he laughed out loud. It's the only time I ever heard him laugh. The middle part of his body shook with laughter, as it does with short fat men."

Willkie paused.

"What did you do?" I asked.

"I just looked at him. The whole scene appalled me. It was as if I saw him naked.

"When he stopped laughing he trembled a little, but quickly overcame it. He put the cigar back into his mouth, asked me to sit down, said I looked well and how was I anyhow—imitating American speech."

Willkie fell silent and looked at his shoes. He was leaning back in his chair with his feet on the desk.

"What happened then?" I asked.

Willkie took his feet off the desk and sat up. He did not answer my question, but said: "This is all off-the-record of course. Churchill is working for Britain—"

"For Tory Britain," I put in.

"Naturally," said Willkie and put his feet back onto the desk. "What else could one expect him to be doing? Britain—Tory and otherwise—is up against it in more ways than one. His job is simple. He's the only man the British have—"

"The British Tories have," I said.

184   "All right. He's the only man the British Tories

have who may be able to pull off the job—and he's
pulling it. He's out to get us to underwrite the
British Empire. Nothing else. And he's succeeding."

Willkie told the wheelchair story at some length
to at least two other people I know and briefly
before a number of small groups in and around
New York during the last half of 1943 when he
was trying to line up the Republican nomination
in '44. Apparently he considered it very significant,
a revelation of an important element in international politics which he heartily disliked, believing it a barrier to his One World idea.

When asked what he thought of Churchill's insistence that monarchies must be restored in Greece
and Yugoslavia, Willkie replied with great vehemence, "If that's what we are fighting for, I want to
quit right now."

I saw him once more soon after his overwhelming
defeat in the Wisconsin primaries, following which
he withdrew as a candidate for the Republican
nomination. He was very subdued and had little to
say.

It looked almost certain that the Republicans
would nominate Thomas E. Dewey. I asked Willkie if he would support him.

"I . . . I suppose I'll give him a perfunctory
endorsement in order to stay in the party."

I said I would vote for Roosevelt again.

Willkie nodded dismally.

Toward midsummer 1944 the press made much of a letter Roosevelt had supposedly written to Willkie. Also I heard he had been seeing the President. Everybody was speculating as to whether Willkie would back Roosevelt or Dewey. One rumor had it that F.D.R. did not expect his open support in the election, but was asking for his post-election help toward uniting the liberal, democratic elements within and outside of the Democratic and Republican parties. This would put the Republican Old Guard and the southern-Democrat reactionaries on the run. Still another bit of gossip rumored that Roosevelt wanted Willkie to go as his representative to Germany after the defeat of the Nazis and take charge of American policy there.

Willkie and I had a luncheon engagement for September 6. That morning his secretary phoned me canceling it: Willkie wasn't feeling well.

"Nothing serious, I hope," I said.

"No," she replied. "I think just too much Indiana fried chicken."

A few days later the press reported that Willkie was in hospital. Early on Sunday, October 9, I turned on the radio and heard he had died that morning.

The news almost numbed me.

—This puts a big hole in the world.

I did not again see F.D.R. up close. Toward the end of the 1944 campaign, I heard him speak at the Foreign Policy Association dinner in New York. I borrowed a friend's opera glasses: he did not look well. Earlier that day he had ridden for hours in a heavy drizzle through Manhattan and Brooklyn to disprove the Republican whispers of his ill health. And that night his speech, although it had more than all of Dewey's put together, was pretty much a campaign piece.

But I voted for him. There was no alternative. Dewey was on record as favoring a straight combination of "the English-speaking nations." That sort of thing seemed poison to me. With Roosevelt, there might . . . just might be a chance.

When in February 1945 I saw the newsreels of the Big Three at the Yalta conference, I was shocked at Roosevelt's appearance.

—Here in this man sitting between Churchill and Stalin, so jaunty in '42, now barely holding himself up in his chair, is a summation of the American tragedy of these past few years. Its chief actor is a sick, defeated man. Quite likely what has crept upon him is as much psychological as physical. That he's folded up in his role is not only his own down-going, but a wider human tragedy—American and world tragedy. It's not his fault alone that he's succumbing; it's everybody's —particularly ours in America. We have no better man. We'd not have tolerated a better man. Even he is hated by millions of us, not for his worst qualities but for his best. . . .

Somehow in the movie theater that evening it did not occur to me that he might soon die. But my feelings about him became consistently tender.

His report on Yalta, delivered to a joint session of Congress, was full of impatience with the small nations. He hadn't a good word for any of them and revealed no appreciation of what was happening in people's souls in the backward countries. But I was no longer critical.

—The emperor has aged. He's tired, bone-tired. Probably ill. The whole huge international problem has come to be a burden to him. A terrible burden. . . . "Peace" is about to break out and we're no more prepared for peace than we were for the war.

There was a frantic note in the part of the speech that dealt with the forthcoming United Nations Conference in San Francisco. It was quite evident that now all his eggs were in that basket. He wanted the conference to begin at once. He had insisted on the earliest possible date to Stalin, who apparently was in no great hurry.

Perhaps it was symbolically appropriate that the spring was early and that by mid-April lilacs were

blooming in many dooryards over the grieving
land.

Lincoln too died before the job was done. His
leadership, perhaps less perfect in actuality than
it later seemed, saved the Union. It gave the people
a chance to make the United States a great and
good place. The people have never taken full advantage of that chance.

Franklin Roosevelt's leadership, perhaps less
imperfect in actuality than it may appear to history, saved the country. It also helped to save the
world from being overwhelmed by what is the
worst in it. It helped to give the better side of it
a chance to get hold of itself—to organize, assert
itself—to achieve national and international expression—to give meaning to the history in the
making.

PART IV

LEGACIES AND INHERITANCE TAXES

CHAPTER XIV

One World or No World

IT WAS not in Franklin Delano Roosevelt's nature to want to make his country over, let alone the world. He worked with, on and for the country and the world as he found them.

His Presidency probably was as well motivated as it could be under the circumstances which converged upon his personality in mounting complexity and insistence. It frequently looked, and probably was, brilliant. Its momentary results often were impressive. Their sum-total cannot yet be seen.

This much is sure: Roosevelt's leadership yanked the United States out of a terrible predicament which he recognized while most of the country was still mainly unaware of it. He left the American people another opportunity—perhaps the last —to make this favored land between two oceans a great and good place. And his leadership was one of the forces holding out a chance—perhaps the last—to other peoples to improve, with our aid and the world's cooperation, their sections of the earth.

The United Nations appears to have been chiefly

F.D.R.'s idea. At any rate, he made it his own.
It is the most valuable item in his legacy. Perhaps history will phrase his ultimate epitaph
on the basis of whether or not it becomes a firm
reality.

Franklin Roosevelt counted on its becoming
reality.

It may be that in the final years he thought of
everything else as of transient importance—including his playing along with the unadmirable qualities of American life, appeasing aggressive reaction,
tolerating the "men of the moment" about him,
standing too close to Winston Churchill. Time—*if*
atom bombs or "atomic poison gas" or "biological
dust" don't wipe us all out—will tell whether he
was right.

His vivid, large personality, his bubbling ego
discouraged the development of other leaders.

Too often, American-fashion, F.D.R. improvised, acted only at the last moment. By the
time he initiated the calling of the San Francisco
Conference he was a dying man.

And a year after he was brought to the rose
garden at Hyde Park, the United Nations is not
yet a firm reality. On the contrary, it is no more
than a forum for petty bickering over rules of

procedure, over issues raised by men intent on disguising actual attitudes, problems, dilemmas, as well as spiritual and intellectual bankruptcy. Few of the members of the various UN councils are capable of sincerity. The insincerity of one ex- tenuates the insincerity of the other.

This—the most obvious—aspect of the United Nations is in substantial part a consequence of the United States' wartime policies and behavior. So are other dangerously negative phases of the situation which engulfs us in 1946—and nearly everything about that situation is negative.

. . . Soon after the far-flung football game ended in victory for our side, our team began to disintegrate before the eyes of the world which had expected so much from us. The technical name for what happened in the United States armed forces, notably in the Army, during the winter of 1945-1946 is "mutiny," but the new Commander-in-Chief and the generals and admirals dared not call it that; it was backed by the people at home. . . .

. . . The man whom F.D.R. in his decline had approved as his potential successor was seized with a desperate desire to return the country to what his counterpart in 1920 had called "normalcy." That impulse swung into full play directly after V-J Day. The new White House tenant had to drug his sense of inadequacy by gaining popular favor if but for a moment. The recrudescence of hope and the redoubling of effort among American lookers-backward is one result. The 1946 famine in Europe and Asia is another. . . .

. . . Naming a super-airplane-carrier for Franklin Delano Roosevelt was the first prominent gesture to perpetuate his name. . . .

. . . Eleven months after his "dear friend's" death, Winston Churchill, escorted by the new President whom he soon called Harry, journeyed to Fulton, Missouri, implicitly to dismiss the United Nations idea as nonsense, explicitly to call for an immediate "English-speaking" alliance. And in the name of Christianity and civilization he all but urged an immediate atom-bomb attack on the USSR. After his speech he was fêted by eminent Americans, many of whom as I write in June 1946 still think—and say among themselves—that the former Prime Minister of Great Britain and his ideas deserve the most sympathetic consideration. The blunt and logical among them go so far as to say (actual words of a high-ranking general): "Now is the time to blow those Communist bastards off the face of the earth. . . ."

. . . A year after F.D.R.'s death, his successor made ex-President Herbert Hoover his special envoy to the famine-stricken countries of Europe and Asia. In doing this President Truman was either ignorant or unmindful of the fact—well known in Russia—that the following, which appeared in John Barry's column "Ways of the World" in the August 13, 1931, San Francisco News, was never denied:

"President Hoover I know very well.* One day at the Department of Commerce, I had an intimate talk with him. The subject of Russia came up. Hoover said: 'To tell the truth, Marsh, the ambition of my life is to crush out Soviet Russia.'"

. . . Two weeks after F.D.R. was abundantly eulogized on the first anniversary of his death, Walter Lippmann, the careful observer-analyst, returned from a trip to the devastated continent of Europe and reported on May 4 as his "most important conclusion . . . that all European governments, all parties, and all leading men are acting as *if* there would be another war. There are some who dread it, some who want it, some who think it is inevitable, some who think it can be averted. But with no exceptions among those who form policy in Europe . . . the ultimate and determining calculation is that . . . they must act as if there were going to be another war." Three days later Lippmann reported another conclusion: that "the American government is basically uninformed"

* Barry was here quoting a conversation Hoover had had with Benjamin Marsh, head of the People's Lobby in Washington.

about the situation and "has lost touch with the realities." Much of this, in Lippmann's view, is traceable to the wartime squabbles over the Second Front and the set of political motivations which underlay Allied war operations. . . .

. . . In the United States, three opinion polls conducted between January and May 1946 indicated that from seventy to seventy-seven per cent of the people were expecting a war—with Russia —within twenty years. . . . In the same period the K.K.K. revived, anti-Semitism increased; New York City dumped enough food into garbage cans every day to feed two hundred thousand starving people in Europe or Asia; the most vicious sort of anti-British feeling came out into the open; capital-labor and intra-labor crises burst upon the country. "Labor feels that its proper rights can be obtained only through strikes," said Dr. Bryn J. Hovde of the New School for Social Research in the April *American Journal of Economics and Sociology.* "Management feels that to open its books to a public fact-finding commission is tantamount to socialization; houses for veterans of the wars against fascist vermin and slum vermin are unbuilt because there is no people's program; all want the line held firmly against inflation but the OPA is publicly whipped every day by special groups who want the law dropped for themselves. . . ."

. . . The January 2, 1946, issue of the *Christian Century* magazine protested against the "imperialist trap" in the Pacific, the Middle East, Africa, China and Latin America into which Washington was taking the American people, a procedure which could result only in war. . . . While American and British statesmen and their journalistic fellow-travelers fulminated against "Russia's Communist expansionism" and "Red imperialism," the Leftist London newsletter *The Week* reported on May 10 that "the United States armed forces have become lodged in fifty-six countries and islands in which they were not situated before the war. . . . American bases are being built in Iceland and Saudi Arabia, distant respectively 3,500 and 7,000 miles from the nearest United States frontier. A Soviet equivalent would be bases in Greenland and Venezuela." . . .

. . . On May 14 the New York *Herald Tribune* editorialized on the schizophrenia within the State Department, which it called "a monument to nineteenth-century America's sublime disinterest in foreign policy," and suggested that something ought to be done toward acquiring a foreign policy. The country "can hardly do without one forever. . . ." Said the *New Republic* of May 20: "Symbolically, our foreign policy rests on three generals—Francisco Franco, Chiang Kai-shek and Leslie Groves. These are three wobbly reeds. Franco and Chiang are sure to be ousted from their ruling positions. *Dinner* Groves makes new enemies for America every *at the* day by manufacturing more and more [atomic] *White House* bombs. . . ."

. . . Said Ralph Ingersoll, ex-army officer, editor of *PM*, author of *Top Secret*, in Madison Square Garden, New York, on May 16, 1946: "There are military men in Washington who have actually told me that they regard you and me as simply on furlough, loaned out by the Army for a little breather before the whole thing begins all over again. Why? I believe that there exists on a world-wide basis a genuine conflict of interests between what the Government of the Soviet Union sees as its security and what the Government of the British Empire sees as its security. Whether or not this conflict will be resolved depends upon the U.S.A. . . . The same conflict existed during the war, when American armed forces had as their objective the defeat of Germany by the quickest and most direct route, while England sought to accomplish this objective only on such terms as would further the political interests of the British Empire. The American point of view won out only because we knew exactly what we wanted and everyone stood fast by the American principle. . . . What I see happening today is that strong forces in America, 200 which have always been against our trying to work out a peaceful relationship with the Russians, have found strong allies abroad. The men who are *Legacies* guiding Britain's foreign policy seem willing to *and* risk even war to get their way. I *don't* say they are *Inheritance* trying to start a war; I *do* say that their policies in- *Taxes* volve the risk. And I think the efforts, on both sides of the Atlantic, to make it appear that a conflict between the United States and the Soviet Union is inevitable are the single most dangerous thing that is happening in the world today. . . . If you do not catch on to the fact that this talk of the 'inevitability of war' is phony—a lie that is purposely told to trick you—then my friends in Washington are right—and you are not out of the Army at all—but only on furlough, sent home for a little rest before—"

A year following the Grand Coalition's complete military defeat of the Axis, the world could not be in a worse condition short of actual military hostilities among its erstwhile members; and there is no doubt that the major causes of that condition existed during the war—at the time of Churchill's first stay in the White House; in June 1942 when Willkie saw F.D.R. and Churchill; at the Quebec, Teheran, Yalta and San Francisco conferences.

The friend whom I have quoted was probably right: the decline of F.D.R.'s spirit and body began at the first Big Three conference. There he really grasped the Enormous Difficulty. It then grasped *Dinner* him. In the desperation of his dying years he must *at the* have placed his last hope in the United Nations— *White House* and in the American people's doing their part toward making it a working reality.

"I have a terrific headache. . . ."

A year after his painful last words Franklin Roosevelt seems to be losing. The American people seem reluctant even to provide—even to sell—an appropriate piece of real estate for the permanent headquarters of the United Nations. America's new leaders, many of whom F.D.R. assisted to high position, are "men of the moment" sprinkled among relics of the past, all looking backward, afraid to look ahead, dancing to emergencies, incapable of welcoming or even accepting the future that insists on coming. Some of them are intent on doing everything in their power to bring on a war with the USSR as soon as possible. Others are resigned to the possibility or probability of such a war.

They are heirs to all that is worst in the prewar and war eras: to suspicion of our most powerful wartime ally, to the policy of catering to our day-to-day appetites and our dislike of restrictions. Many pay lip service to the creative elements in F.D.R.'s speeches and programs, but do nothing to implement them. They are unable to inspire faith 202 in the future and lead the people toward determined, constructive action in the international field.

Most of the new men in power have disclosed no inkling of responsible realization that the crisis, far from ending with V-E and V-J days, has been growing worse; that F.D.R. solved no fundamental problems, but only held them in abeyance; and that, along with the unimplemented United Nations formula, he left us the atomic bomb and other secret weapons—the "biological" kind allegedly even worse than the A-bomb.

The new President and his close "advisers" seem to have no cause, no ideas worthy of being called that, no policy. They are all dressed up but don't know where to go. The A-bomb is the core of their world.

Abroad the USA is feared and hated.

Walt Whitman's "ever-returning spring" has returned once more as I write, and the lilac bushes have bloomed again

> . . . *tall-growing with heart-shaped leaves*
> *of rich green,*
> *With many a pointed blossom rising delicate, with*
> *the perfume strong I love . . .*

And it may be that we are caught in as dark a period as followed the death of Lincoln.

Historians have written of the post-Lincolnian

"Tragic Era," speculating upon what that era might have been had he lived. He would have treated the South intelligently, generously. His leadership would have precluded carpetbagging. It would have tried to create a decent basis for White-Negro relations. It would have moderated the scramble for self-seeking advantage that came on the heels of the War Between the States.

Whether or not Lincoln would have tried to do all this is questionable, to say nothing of whether the people would have let him.

Speculation has already begun as to the directions in which Roosevelt would be leading were he still alive. His prestige is greater in the second year after his death than at almost any time in his life. Ironically, and in a way naturally, it grows as the possibility of achieving what seemed to be his best goals shrinks. And politicians, both those who admired him and those who despised him, are exploiting that prestige for petty immediate ends.

One hears people talking: If he were still alive, he might not have dropped the A-bomb on Hiroshima and Nagasaki. He would not have taken Churchill to Fulton. He—

Looking back after his death, and from the present wrongness of events, they wishfully attribute to him the wisdom his heirs so signally lack.

We are a confused people, full of generous impulses and isolative suspicions; most of us still wanting to do what is right, but joining in the *Legacies* scramble for temporary advantages, standing in *and* queues for nylons, telephoning the dealer about *Inheritance* that new car, cursing John L. Lewis, repeating the *Taxes* latest jokes about Harry Truman, preferring Charlie McCarthy to current-events analysts, the best of whom are under surveillance by the agents of the "Rankin Committee" on Un-American Activities.

We are caught between the two chief items of F.D.R.'s legacy. The texture of events demands we pay the inheritance taxes on the legacy, but we don't like to. In fact some of us refuse to. So the atmosphere in which we live is very strange. Nobody likes it. Nobody seems to be able to figure it out satisfactorily to the country at large.

In the midst of a money prosperity "the tensions in this country are greater than they were in the depths of the depression of the last decade," writes Anne O'Hare McCormick in the May 18 New York *Times*. ". . . Against the background of ruin, hunger and awful misery that envelops other peoples and touches us so lightly [these tensions] appear shockingly frivolous, a manifestation of irresponsibility on the part of all concerned that looks almost as if we were bent on doing to ourselves what the war did to less fortunate countries." **205**

It may be that the United States is one of the most *un*fortunate countries.

After a tour of several weeks from New York to California, Samuel Grafton reported in the New York *Post* (June 6, 1946) that "the people of this republic are passing through a bad hour, emotionally." He quoted a Los Angeles woman: "I just want to sit in the patio and put my feet on a chair and drink beer. People are kind of milling around, in a futile way; they don't talk about the atomic age any more, or any other kind of age. They damn the unions mechanically, but without real interest. . . . They don't know what to think. There just doesn't seem to be a voice anywhere in the world; Roosevelt is gone, Willkie is dead. . . . [Ex-servicemen] are in a mood that's hard to understand. . . . It's as if there should have been something wonderful for everybody after the war, and it isn't there. Maybe the wartime ads about the postwar period have backfired."

Is this only the postwar letdown? Or something more fundamental? Grafton quotes a California candidate for Congress: "It is almost as if we had thrown up our hands and had lost faith in ourselves. You still hear political arguments; this is a very articulate community; but it is almost as if there were an inability to focus, and the arguments trail into nothing."

A Canadian journalist, Bruce Hutchison, published an interesting article, "Is the United States Fit To Lead the World?" in the March 1, 1946, *Maclean's* (Toronto), the gist of which is that the American people have lost their bearings and that, if the world is to have a future, they had better recover them soon. Our ideal of the pursuit of happiness "has been distorted beyond recognition of the Founding Fathers." We are not a happy people. Our inner life is a poor thing. We are "dazzled by the paraphernalia of outer happiness, the glittering, thin satisfactions of unexampled luxury which threaten to drug" us. We don't know we are "the hope of the world," but Mr. Hutchison thinks we may wake up before it is too late.

Millions of well-"educated" Americans who used to seem balanced and integrated are suddenly caught in a tangle of personal and supra-personal fears, and are making no effort to cope with their individual problems or to interest themselves in local, national and international affairs and movements. They hear ominous warnings about the absolute crisis facing mankind, and they don't, they can't respond, partly because—as Professor Howard Mumford Jones of Harvard explained in an address early in June 1946—"a genteel education" did not prepare them "to grapple with concepts of this magnitude." Consciously or unconsciously afraid, they do nothing. Even many of those in highly comfortable economic circumstances are dissatisfied, vaguely uncomfortable. Professor Jones believes that these people—millions of them, including many so-called leading people in their communities and in the nation—"no longer believe in the culture which has maintained them," and so "a psychology of fear becomes central" in their lives. "Frightened men are insecure and seek security. Seeking, we may land in a social mysticism as did the Nazi state. . . . We educate the finest engineers and biologists, but our human engineering is so bad that twelve months after victory we don't know what to do with it. . . . While military hospitals are full of human wreckage, irresponsible officials are planning a new world war, although scientists have told us again and again that the use of the bomb on any such scale as ignorant politicians or professional militarists contemplate may extinguish all human life."

Our most determined-seeming actions have to do with the world-wide armament race, in which we are momentarily leading. Bikini was a military maneuver or rehearsal looking ahead to another global war. At the same time (spring and summer of 1946) primary elections in various parts of the United States indicate trends toward isolationism, toward international irresponsibility.

We seem to be rebelling against history which placed more power in our hands than any people ever had. We—the people and the government—don't know what to do with it. We seem to want to default on our obligations. And this makes for uneasiness, fear. The atomic bomb is part of it all. To some of us, the bomb is the core of the psychological plight in which we find ourselves. Some of the Protestant churchmen regard the atomic destruction of Hiroshima and Nagasaki as the greatest atrocities on record. Some of us are asking: Why did President Truman order the use of the A-bomb? Merely to hasten Japan's surrender? Or also, if not chiefly, as a gesture against Russia? Certainly the Russians can suspect the latter. . . . But while questions like these are in the air, coming up together and getting in each other's way, most Americans engage mainly in trivialities. The great majority are at best but superficially informed. They are confused and tend to be disappointed and cynical, and in that state of mind they vote against any candidate who favors more participation in world affairs on the ground that such a man is chasing a phantom. . . . And come Whitman's "ever-returning spring," we pour rivers of printer's ink into eulogies of Franklin Roosevelt instead of into thoughtful discussions of plans for tackling the current major problems.

Legacies and Inheritance Taxes

Efforts to examine critically our failure as a world power are spotty, sporadic.

So there may not be very many more springs to be enjoyed by human beings. The lilacs may not bloom very many more times, nor the roses around F.D.R.'s grave. The earth itself may turn into a tomb.

Not a few of us know this; some of us consider it ironic at a time when the potentialities for creative life in the world—and especially in the United States—are greater than ever before.

Of the two crucial items in F.D.R.'s legacy, it seems very likely that the atomic bomb and the other secret weapons and our attitude toward them will take us into World War III more quickly than the United Nations formula can evolve into an effective technique.

Can this likelihood be reversed rapidly enough?

Of course, whether or not the United Nations can evolve does not depend entirely on the American people. There are many influencing factors outside the USA and beyond our control. But the United Nations cannot function effectively without a vitally interested, democratic United States. The world may have from two to fifteen years in which to make it work; possibly less than two, conceivably more than fifteen. But if we Americans are to do our part a good many of us must start at once —in 1946—coolly and intelligently, with steadily sharpening understanding of why we have failed so far and what we must do to survive.

Churchill's Either-Or alternatives are growing obsolescent. The alternatives now may very well be as simple and final as: One World or No World.

If we choose One World, then—

I

We the people of the United States must take a hard look at ourselves, distill all the sincerity and direction we can from the cross-purposes in our souls, and get behind the United Nations idea with a powerful determination that justice and equality become a perceptible trend here and the world over.

As a beginning, we might do well to read and induce others to read the article in the June 1946 *Harper's* entitled "The Beam in Our Own Eye," by Clyde Eagleton, professor of international law at New York University, who worked on the UN Charter for two years in the State Department and served as a technical expert with the United States delegation at the San Francisco Conference. Dr. Eagleton reminds us that we "deliberately made

[the United Nations Charter] as weak as we could"
in deference to the United States Senate's strong
attachment to American sovereignty, and in opposition to the Russians; that the "veto," which we
denounce so lustily when the Russians practice it,
is one of our own principal devices within the
Security Council; that since the San Francisco Conference the USA's contribution toward international peace has been inferior to that of the USSR;
that when it comes to postwar expansionism we
have surpassed the Russians; that we have the atom
bomb; and that the problem of the future of the
UN is not in Russia but in us. "Whatever Russia
wants or does not want," says Professor Eagleton,
"nothing can be done until the American people
make up their minds to a definite and consistent
policy which they are willing to support and for
which they are willing to pay the price. [*My italics*
—L. A.] It is the United States which now blocks
advance toward real security. That is our problem;
the problem of Russia comes later. We are now in
a vicious circle, and there is no use arguing whose
fault it is or who began it; someone must cut
through it. The responsibility for taking the first
steps in this direction is ours: we are the strongest
and most influential state in the world at the moment; the UN cannot be made stronger unless we
do it . . ."

We must cease to insist on remaining a super-privileged country. Current appearances to the contrary, such insistence will not get us anywhere —in the end, we can't remain super-privileged. Such insistence was partly responsible for World War II (to go no farther back) and that war horribly depleted many of our basic natural resources and added a couple of hundred billion dollars to our national debt, while in 1946 we are expected to feed large parts of the world for a long time. A privileged position among nations did not pay in the past; if we continue to insist on it, perhaps to the point of attempting semi-isolation hand in hand with imperialism, there is no end of trouble ahead which can ultimately lead only to war.

This does not mean that we must make a special, conscious effort to reduce our living standards. It means that as a people, as a state, we must make a special conscious effort, through the UN and through the apparatus of our own government, to help raise the living standards of other peoples, other states.

Legacies and Inheritance Taxes

II

We the people of the United States must perceive that nuclear fission can be used not only as a catastrophically destructive weapon of war but as a tremendous boon to man. Its control and the Dinner development of its constructive potentiality must at the be put within a firmly established United Nations White House Organization heading toward a world federation, a world government.

III

We the people of the United States must press the government into formulating and practicing a foreign policy which will fit into an effective United Nations apparatus and encourage democracy at home and (not necessarily like ours; in some respects, perhaps preferably unlike ours) in China and Yugoslavia, Russia and Greece, India and Spain, Brazil and Palestine, Indonesia and the Philippines, Nigeria and Britain . . . everywhere.

The future has no room for the idea that the "Anglo-Americans" own a patent on democratic processes.

IV

At the same time we the people of the United States must make ourselves realize that we cannot formulate and practice a firm, intelligent, democratic foreign policy unless we infuse our democracy at home with new vitality and wider scope so *214* that it will satisfy economically, socially, politically, ethnically a larger and growing number of citizens, gradually equalizing our standards of living and raising the quality of our cultural urges and aspirations; and that will bring out new leaders as different from the Trumans and Byrneses, the Leahys and Snyders as day is from night. *Legacies and Inheritance Taxes*

Such a process will embrace eagerness for contact with other peoples, the desire to exchange with them not only material goods but ideas and cultural forms and practices; it will include the concept of One World, and the encouragement of freedom of personal movement here and there, back and forth, everywhere, regardless of color, race, religion and nationality; freedom to mingle and exchange influences.

If we can revive faith in our present economic order and succeed in putting it to work toward such a democracy, well and good. If not, we'd better revise it quickly into something in which we can have faith, or replace it with another system. Said the United States Committee for Economic Development: "The present [1946] situation has in it all the ingredients of another 1929 boom and collapse." The Kiplinger *Washington Letter* (May 4, 1946), "circulated privately to businessmen," predicted that prosperity was ahead, then most likely a bust. This is the feeling of most business leaders and most publications which reflect or cater to their "thinking." They have no real faith in the system whose main processes they control. The "bust" they expect will bring mass unemployment, but they shout "Communist!" at advocates of public-works programs arranged in advance of depressions. Politically they are in the main anti-"Communist," *not pro*-democratic. They are chiefly anti-Russian, *not pro*-American. They are bent on proving Goebbels right. Some are regretting that we destroyed Germany, our natural ally against Russia. Most of them appear to be incapable of learning anything.

"Ah," you say, "but this is human nature" [further quoting Dr. Hovde]. "But we fought the war to preserve our freedom to make mistakes." . . . A democracy, especially the democracy that has to make decisions as important as those now confronting America, ought to derive greater benefits from a terrible war than the right to live in confusion. It ought not only to be free; it should be competent to deal with the problems of peace in a manner both constructive and orderly. Differences of opinion will always exist, but democracy must be mature enough, intelligent enough to apply the same self-discipline and energy and agreement to the problems of organizing for peace as it did in organizing itself for war.

We cannot establish productive friendly relations with other powers—relations whose atmosphere, functioning and ultimate goal are such as to make our internal processes more compatible with

those of other countries and theirs with ours—unless we do organize our country into a dynamic Legacies
democracy inexorably bent on raising the chances *and*
for a good life of a rapidly increasing number of *Inheritance*
people—a good life in terms of food, shelter, cloth- *Taxes*
ing, spirit-enlarging education, enjoyment of lei-
sure.

If a democracy is dynamic, it means that a great
many individuals living in it consistently take an
active part in its diverse workings. Incidentally,
this sort of activity would expand the creative side
of our character and personality.

We need to ask ourselves what is wrong with a
political, economic, social system that cannot meet,
say, the 1946 housing crisis, although we have the
money, the material, the machinery and the know-
how.

We must each of us decide whether elected
officials or elective candidates are working for or
against an expanding democracy at home and a
firm, constructive policy abroad. We must be ruth-
lessly insistent that our elected leaders carry out
our wishes. If they do not, they must be replaced.
The machinery which now exists for replacing
them should be studied, perhaps rebuilt and made
more quickly operative—as it is, for example, in
Britain.

The United States Congress has long been extremely inefficient. Even its progressive members

work unsatisfactorily, under overpowering handicaps. Too much of their time is taken up with committee hearings, investigations; with political trivialities. Perhaps little can be done about the latter: a politician must keep his ears to the ground, his fences mended. Perhaps we need a fourth branch of the government, called, say, the National Council, consisting, like the Supreme Court, of nine life-tenure members selected from the best minds in the country. Its duties would be to discern, investigate, analyze and report on trends and tides in our national life and our relations with the rest of the world. It would be a nonpartisan prestige body, charged with the function of submitting recommendations for action to the President and his administrative departments, to Congress and the people. Its setup, budget and staffs would enable it to conduct many investigations simultaneously, rapidly and efficiently. It would not be an answer to all our prayers, but would make for more governmental and public intelligence than the present system of Congressional committees and sporadically appointed President's commissions.

In the last analysis, political power in the United States, and therefore the power to change what we don't like in our economic and social conditions, lies in the hands of the people. What kind of leaders we have, what kind and extent of democracy we have, is up to the voting populace: the house- wife cooking dinner, the factory hand tightening bolts, the farmer planting corn, the proprietor of the country store who doubles as town council- man, the student doing postgraduate work and the professor who teaches him. It is up to the beauty-shop operator and her bridge-playing or career-woman clients, to the stevedore loading a ship and the captain who commands it. How this country is run is up to every single person who casts a vote on Election Day, and no amount of alibis or buck-passing relieves a single one of us from our responsibility for the way we are governed.

Too many of us are scared stiff by that nebulous force called public opinion. If we have a criticism of prevailing institutions, or a suggestion for their alteration and improvement, we hesitate to speak up, afraid that our remarks will get us in bad with the community. Consequently we don't discover the other people in our neighborhood who may be seeing things much as we do.

The vociferous clamor many of us emit over trivialities or in hasty superficial reaction to serious events or in defense of sectional interests sets up such a cacophonous din that thoughtful and more pertinent clamor isn't heard or listened to.

As individuals or as members of local groups

whether small or large, Americans must not be discouraged or diverted from our purpose because radio, press, church and school—the widest public media of communication—are timid about clamoring for anything approaching dynamic democracy. These media are now largely controlled by people and groups whose interests keep them on the side which does not further freedom, equality and general welfare. But the mails and telegraph wires are still free; most adult Americans have the vote, and most legislators and elective officials are sensitive to public opinion—and public opinion is what we make it.

Yell! But time your yelling. Inform yourself before you yell. Yell in concrete day-to-day terms for a dynamic long-range democratic process as defined above.

Most of our public prints interpret the principle of the freedom of the press as freedom to suppress news and intelligent interpretation of events. Insist on getting full information.

V

We the people of the United States will have to see that, as world democracy grows and the empire system dwindles, the overpopulated British Isles receive such help as they will need and we and other sources, notably the free dominions, can give in the course of their readjustment toward a level of equality with other peoples. It does not follow that the British people sink to the level of the Albanians, say, or the Burmese; the idea is to help hoist the Albanians and Burmese up. No nation, however, should be aided which tolerates a government, whether labeled Tory or socialist, whose purpose or function it is to hold the Albanians and Burmese down. Nor should the American people tolerate a government, whether labeled Republican or Democrat, which helps another government to hold them down. We must not permit our officials in Washington to underwrite repression.

VI

We the people of the United States need to realize that potentially or actually the USSR and the USA are equally great powers, and that friendship between the two is essential to both and to the world in general.

We must delve into the whys and wherefores of the Russians' suspicions of the West, just as they should delve into the West's suspicions of them. If but a portion of what Michael Sayers and Albert E. Kahn set forth in their book *The Great Conspiracy: The Secret War Against the Soviet Union*

(1946) is true, it is no wonder that the Russians are suspicious.

We must expect from the Soviet Union understanding and fair judgment about our country; we must speak and write about the USSR with the same degree of fairness. Reciprocity is essential to any successful relationship.

Early in 1946 Scott Nearing suggested that Americans now unintentionally working for World War III might head in the other direction by trying the shoe on the other foot:

If the Soviet Union possessed the secret of the atomic bomb and were doing its best to keep it from us, meanwhile building up a stockpile of the bombs, maintaining an army larger than ever before in its history and a navy larger than all the other navies of the world combined, proposing to continue the wartime draft and introduce universal compulsory military training in time of so-called peace, allowing her Army and Navy officers to talk openly of attacking us before we should have time to recover from our war effort and perhaps learn to make our own atomic bombs, carrying on a press and radio campaign to foment suspicion and hostility toward us, seizing and holding military bases along both our frontiers (Iceland, Greenland, the islands of the Pacific), sending a naval expedition into northern waters for special training in arctic warfare, maintaining armed forces at our very gates (United States Marines, planes and ships in Manchuria, United

States troops and anti-Soviet armies in India, Germany,
Italy, Greece), proposing for 1947—two years after the
war—a military budget greater than that of any other
country, with a higher percentage of expenditure for
military purposes than was made by Germany or Japan
when they were actively preparing for war, and if the
Greek Orthodox Church were offering to lead a holy
war against us and if Marshal Stalin officially sponsored
a public ceremony at which a former Prime Minister
who had twice tried to overthrow our Government
and our economic system was highly honored and in
his address urged an alliance between our two most
powerful rivals—what would they think of Generalis-
simo Truman and Foreign Commissar Byrnes if they
did not work night and day to see that the United
States had friendly governments in every capital from
Canada to Argentina, and if they did not move heaven
and earth to discover the secret of the atomic bomb?

VII

To gain time to get going on something re-
sembling the six points listed above, to gain time
for the United Nations to develop so it may nip
off World War III, we the people of the United
States must force our 1946 leaders to take prompt
steps toward effecting an ideological compromise
—or at least a truce—on the international scene. It
is necessary primarily between the United States

and the Soviet Union, but it should extend to
Dinner countries like Greece and Poland.

at the We won't bring about such a compromise or
White House truce, unless we Americans realize that, partly
owing to our lack of a positive democratic orientation toward the backward countries, and to nature's abhorrence of a vacuum, Soviet ideology has
seeped into some parts of the world. There is nothing we can do about it—not any more—unless we
want to follow up Churchill's hints and atom-
bomb out of existence the vital centers of the
USSR, eastern Europe and new China. As already
suggested, there are people in the United States
who are ready to do this, but I assume that Americans in general are not.

Our best practical course for the near future,
until we can actualize some of the difficult pre-con-
ditions of lasting peace, is to face two facts: first,
that, having failed to develop a democratic foreign policy during and immediately after the war,
we have politically precious little at present to offer
the peoples of the undeveloped countries; second,
that we have much to offer toward their industrial
improvement. We can take them our wonderful
technology and with that equipment and "know-
how," and our friendly, informal personal behavior, we can make friends and influence people
while we are earning a reasonable return on our
224 money.

This is no new idea: it's a couple of years old at least. It is not entirely unheard of even in the State Department. F.D.R. may have entertained it occasionally. In October 1944 the politician in him said: "I intend to find jobs for sixty million Americans by trebling our exports."

In April 1942 the French political leader Pierre Cot said before the American Association for Social Security: "The Soviet Union, China, the colonial peoples have the same right as America to contribute to the organization of a new Europe. This new organization will be the result of a compromise between the different conceptions of the world which exist today—with the exception of the Fascist conception."

Also in April 1942 the then Soviet Ambassador to the U.S.A., Maxim Litvinoff, said: "Russian Communism will be modified, American democracy will be modified, British capitalism will be modified, as a result of the war. The things that have stood between them will be broken down. The changes in them will bring them closer together. Life is a series of changes. It is a series of throwing away things that are no longer needed or useful."

I know that the idea of an international ideological truce or compromise intrigued Wendell Willkie.

I know too that it is extremely appealing to postwar Yugoslavia, which is rich in natural resources but needs financing, machinery and expert technological and organizational aid. A shrewd American businessman of my acquaintance is convinced that he can help the Yugoslavs raise their living standards if he is permitted to set up dozens of industrial enterprises which—his initial consideration—would make a profit within a few years. All he needs is contracts to buy the materials here and build the plants there. All the Yugoslav government needs to give contracts to Americans like this is an American loan, most of which would be spent here and all of which would be paid back within the agreed period.

This idea was clearly stated on October 11, 1944, by Dr. William G. Carleton of the University of Florida in a paper entitled "The Convergence of the American and Russian Systems" and read before the Southern Council on International Relations at Chapel Hill, North Carolina:

. . . [The tides in Europe and Asia] are ideologically moving in the direction of Russia. The trend . . . is to the Left. . . . Even before 1914 the middle classes were being destroyed in Europe because of the cartelization of business. Since 1914 this trend has been revolutionary in its sweep. . . . This swing to the Left will continue with or without Russian encouragement.

[The Russians] have certain advantages in colonial and backward countries. For one thing, they profess racial equality. More, they practice it. They are not self-conscious in the presence of colored people. . . .

On the other hand, our record at home on the race question is regarded by the outside world as bad. . . .*

For another thing, the Soviet Government has never practiced imperialism in the old sense. When they come to the borders of a backward people, the Russians say in effect: "We do not come to exploit you. We come to help you and to raise your standard of living. . . ." Now it will be difficult to convince some Americans and some Britons that this is not imperialism, but the Russians honestly think it is not imperialistic and there is much evidence that the colonial peoples do not regard it as imperialism. . . .

Moreover, the Russian social and economic system will appeal strongly to backward peoples. Not only will Russian achievements appear tremendous to them, but the Russian methods of accomplishing those achievements are possible for backward peoples in a way that American methods are not.

When the Russians come to a backward people they say in effect: "You want modern industries and mass production . . . modern technology . . . mines and factories and railroads and hydro-electric plants. You have no native capitalist class and no native middle

* In the May 18 and 25, 1946, issues of the *New Yorker* magazine John Hersey reported on the United States Navy officers' and men's contemptuous behavior toward Chinese soldiers.

class to finance the giant industries of today. You do not want to depend on private foreign investors [or] on absentee capitalists [or] on foreign governments. Well, why don't you do as we did? . . . We built those giant industries collectively through government agencies. *True, we called in technicians from foreign countries to help us.* [My italics here and below.—L.A.] . . . When the industries were completed they belonged to us, the people, collectively, and not to foreign capitalists."

Take note that the Russians . . . show that their achievements are within the reach of all backward peoples. They show backward peoples how industrialization can be accomplished in backward countries by the backward people themselves. They do not have to *do* anything or risk anything themselves. They merely have to plant the ideas and to tell the backward peoples to follow their example.

Now we Americans will have no difficulty proving the excellence of our system, certainly as exemplified by our technology and our productive achievements. But we will have a difficult time showing foreign peoples and backward peoples how to attain our system under modern conditions in a day of expensive and centralized technology. . . . How can the economic and social conditions in North America which for several hundred years have made possible the gradual development of this American system be duplicated in Europe today? How can they be duplicated in Asia? Could they be duplicated even in North America today if we had to begin almost from scratch to develop modern technology, as the Chinese and Hindus must do? . . .

Foreigners would be glad to imitate the American [industrial and business methods] if they could see how their own indigenous conditions would make it possible. But they do not see how it is possible. Hence while native parties arise seeking to imitate the Russian way, native parties do not arise seeking to imitate the American way. In other words, if America is to have great influence on the internal development of backward countries, say China for instance, we must *do* something. Native parties will not arise spontaneously to do it for us.

And what can we do? We can go to the backward peoples and say in effect: "We know you want modern mass production and technology. We know you have no native capitalist or middle class to finance the building of these industries. We know that you do not want to be dependent on or to be exploited by foreign investors and absentee capitalists. Besides, private capital in this day of revolt against imperialism, in this day of turmoil and upheaval and revolution, is too timid to venture on its own the building of these great projects. Therefore, the American government will make loans to your government, and help your government build them. . . ."

Now the backward country may object to this on the score that it leaves that country dependent on the government which thus lends a helping hand. And the country which offers it may find widespread opposition at home to such a policy. Americans will say, "Why should we help build industries in China with our money?" American vested interests will say, "Why should we build steel mills in China to compete with steel made in America?" *Now the answer is that if the Chinese millions can be made through industrialization to increase enormously their effective wants, American business will profit immensely.* But many Americans will not see this. . . .

Have we Americans, then, no advantage? To be sure. *As individuals we are, I think, tremendously popular in the world. Other peoples admire our vitality, our push, our breezy independence.* We have, to use Willkie's words, a great reservoir of good will throughout the world. We have never been imperialistic in quite the sense the British, the French, the Germans, and the Italians have been imperialistic. And we stand preeminent in the world in technology and mass production. . . .

Our State Department must become more realistic. Bureaucrats, conventional minds, stuffed shirts, and dilettantes playing socialites at milady's tea can no longer be trusted to conduct our foreign relations. It is not enough to be able to mouth platitudes about "justiciable questions" and "most favored nation" clauses. Men who conduct our foreign affairs must be cognizant of the realities of social politics as it is now being played in Europe and Asia. Remember, our diplomats must henceforth deal more and more with foreign offices staffed with tough-minded realists who came up through labor movements and revolutionary ferment. These men will know their dialectics, and they will also know the world. . . .

In this perplexing world situation, what can we as individuals do? . . . We can help acquaint our fellow Americans with the nature of the forces now gaining strength in Europe and Asia, so that we can deal intelligently with these forces and not merely oppose them by blind reaction, as the Fascist powers did.

The reactionary-fearful or "practical" argument against this, which Professor Carleton did not ignore in his lecture, runs something like this: "What! Lend them money, help them build their industries, to be faced some years hence by a developed country which will side with Russia in a war against us? Nothing doing!" And within its frame this argument has a point, for if our political thinking doesn't keep up with the rest of the world's we *will* go to war. It is not in the cards that the backward parts of the world will reverse their current trend which demands that backwardness be liquidated.

It must be liquidated not only for the sake of the backward countries but for the sake of the highly industrialized United States. Our American reactionaries fail to recognize a most obvious fact —that other industrialized countries, such as

Britain, Canada, France, Czechoslovakia, formerly Germany, do buy vastly more from us than do China and other undeveloped, noncompeting lands.

Senator Claude Pepper of Florida appears to realize this. In his speech, "An American Policy for Peace and a New World," delivered in the Senate on March 20, 1946, he recognized that close economic collaboration among American technology and productivity, the United States Government (supplying loans) and countries which have gone Left in order to extricate themselves from industrial backwardness is all-important to what he considers sound economic, social and political conditions in the United States and the rest of the world:

. . . We cannot have full employment in America, we cannot have the full use of our facilities in agriculture or industry, unless we have great markets all over the world. Conversely, the torn fabric of the world's economy cannot be repaired without our aid and support.

We know there cannot be peace, except upon a stable economic base in the world. Economic war will lead to a shooting war. But economic collaboration among the nations of the world will lead not only to peace but to prosperity.

For the United States, economic isolationism is as

dangerous as political isolationism. To deny a loan for useful purposes reasonably within a nation's ability to repay, is as dangerous to the security of the United States as it was to deny a nation essential to our defense in war, lend-lease.

. . . We cannot afford not to make such a loan, for it is our goods which these loans will buy, our factories they will keep in production, our workers they will employ, our farmers for whom they will provide markets. . . .

They need such a loan to buy in this country the heavy machinery required to start their industries again, the farm machinery needed for their fields, the rolling stock for their railroads, the electrical equipment for their power plants, the machinery with which to open their mines. . . .

To deny that loan because we fear Russia or hate communism means that we drive Russia to tightening instead of liberalizing her economy, to restricting instead of extending the liberties and the living standards of her people, and that we force her to the conclusion that we will never be her real friend, and her future must be made only through her own strength and her own separate way. Nor do we aid our own heavy industries and the workers in them by such blind substitution of prejudice for reason. Wise leadership on our part in the field of economic collaboration will lead not only to our prosperity and our peace but to the development of the backward areas of the earth by enterprising businessmen from this and other lands and to lifting up the major part of the whole human family. . . .

Once we have removed the fear of war and the fear of want, knowledge and culture will flow in ever-expanding streams to all parts of the earth. Then the Social and Economic Council of the United Nations Organization will really begin to function and become the booster pump for the further extension of all human knowledge and skills, scientific and artistic. With the body of knowledge the human race now has, and favorable conditions for its expansion, the magnificence of the edifice we can raise to the human mind and spirit surpasses the imagination.

What stands in the way of an ideological compromise or truce which would lead, through exchange of ideas and practices, to a convergence of the American and Russian systems? What stands in the way of the United States becoming a dynamic democracy? What bars the probability of even so much as an immediate truce on the international scene while we catch our breath and decide which way we want to go? A somewhat superficial but I think true answer is: inertia. It is easier to stay in the same groove, even though we suspect it may lead to annihilation, than to figure out a better one.

Americans do not like war. But which do they dislike most: war, or the amount of mental and spiritual effort involved in trying to prevent it? Be-

234

cause democracy places responsibility on the individual—all individuals living within it—it is the *Legacies* most difficult, the most demanding, of all schemes *and* of human relationships. It is also the most reward- *Inheritance* ing; it has the most to contribute to both the *Taxes* human body and the human spirit. But we have to work for it, and what is more, we have to care about it—care whether we develop it or not. If we care enough, nothing in the world can keep us from attaining it. If we don't care enough—if we continue to slide along on inertia—nothing in the world will give it to us. The Enormous Difficulty confronting us cannot evaporate as though by enchantment.

The Enormous Difficulty is compounded of hard and horrible facts. For example: the Bagdad newspaper *Saut-el-Ahali* ("Voice of the People") gives the following picture of life in Iraq in 1944:

> . . . 90 per cent of the entire population of Iraq live on a subhuman level. They are condemned to a life of starvation and exposed to the ravages of epidemics without benefit of any medical assistance. And these intolerable, primitive conditions exist in the twentieth century among our own Iraqi people, who sweat and toil to make the soil yield riches which are then entirely consumed by others. . . . The government [which operates within the orbit of imperial Britain] has done nothing either to mitigate the distress or combat its causes.

Essentially, this is the picture of lands inhabited by over half of the human race. It is not pleasant to contemplate. A most important part of it is the revolutionary insistence upon change. If we Americans permit our officials to resist it, it means war.

The seven-point program I have outlined—or something like it—would require a lot of active interest and hard work on the part of a lot of Americans. I believe that some such program—which starts in men's minds and ends in their action—is absolutely necessary if the world (of which the United States is a considerable part) is to weather the present situation and prevent an atomic and "biological" war.

But what are the chances that enough Americans will be enough concerned about the situation to do anything about it quickly enough? As already suggested, perhaps very slim. Howard Mumford Jones might point to the deep cultural disintegration in American life, on which I have quoted him, and say that the chances for a quick change in the present American psychology are practically non-existent.

In 1946 the United States has a few Claude Peppers, James Murrays, Wayne Morses, Harley Kilgores and Glen Taylors to dozens of "Senator Claghorns" who call themselves Republicans or Democrats but are indistinguishable.

There are such organizations as the National
Citizens' Political Action Committee, the CIO- *Legacies*
PAC, the Independent Citizens' Committee of the *and*
Arts, Sciences and Professions, the American Coun- *Inheritance*
cil on Race Relations, the Southern Conference *Taxes*
for Human Welfare, the Urban League, the Association for the Advancement of Colored People,
the American Veterans Committee, Woman's Action Committee, the Society of Atomic Scientists,
the Federal Council of the Churches of Christ, the
Institute of Ethnic Affairs, the United Committee
of South-Slavic Americans, East and West Association, the Institute of Pacific Relations, and the National Council of American-Soviet Friendship;*
there are the progressive labor unions in the CIO
and AFL; there are countless women's clubs and
other local bodies, such as the United Nations
Council of Philadelphia; but organizations working in opposition to these, bent on bringing out the
worst in us, are bigger and in possession of very
much vaster resources. The shallow men in the
government more readily follow the wishes of the
latter than the former. The organizations I have
listed and others, now piddling along in their diverse liberal or progressive ways, should get together on general aims—as for instance National

* I mention only organizations with which I am connected or
otherwise familiar.—*L. A.*

237

Citizens' Political Action Committee and the Independent Citizens' Committee of the Arts, Sciences and Professions got together in the spring of 1946. Most of these organizations, including and particularly labor unions, should show more interest in foreign affairs than they have shown in 1945 and the first half of 1946.

Possibly 1948 will be our last political opportunity.

There is need of intelligent militancy.

There is need of about ten million committees of one who will go to work in 1946 and 1947 according to their abilities and, insisting on militancy, will tend toward co-operation with each other, toward merging into larger and larger, more and more dynamic bodies and movements.

There is need of independent voters' movements, such as the one that sprang up in Lynn, Massachusetts, in the spring of 1946.

There is need of thousands of big-city and small-town discussion forums with a national headquarters, something like the old Chautauqua system, which will train and send out speakers to inform the people and encourage them to thrash out the issues and so help pull the country out of the spiritual-political stagnation into which it sank with the war's end. The National Citizens' PAC school which began to train people for militant political work in June 1946 is a step in the right direction.

It may be impossible, even inconceivable, that the United States will bestir itself sufficiently and in time. If the recent past and the present are indicative of the future, there is scant hope. As Professor Eagleton, among others, has suggested, the future depends greatly on the American people.

Eminent persons, persons with audiences, should speak out as often as possible in the manner of Dr. Albert Einstein, who on May 29, 1946—when asked, "Is not human nature an invincible obstacle to reaching permanent peace?"—said:

"Now many will say that fundamental agreement with Russia is impossible under the present circumstances. Such a statement would be justified if the United States had made a serious attempt in this direction during the last year. I find, however, that the opposite has happened. There was no need to accept Fascist Argentina into the United Nations against Russia's opposition. There was no need to manufacture new atomic bombs without letup and to appropriate $12,000,000,000 for defense in a year in which no military threat was to be expected for the near future. Nor was it necessary to delay the proposed measures against Franco Spain.

"It is senseless to recount here the details which

all show that nothing has been done in order to alleviate Russia's distrust, a distrust which can very well be understood in the light of the events of the last decades and to whose origin we contributed not a little.

"A permanent peace cannot be prepared by threats but only by the honest attempt to create mutual trust. One should think that the wish to create a decent form of life on this planet and to avert the danger of unspeakable destruction would tame the passions of responsible men. You cannot rely on that. . . . The only hope . . . lies in the securing of peace in a supernatural way."

Universities, colleges, schools, churches, clubs, libraries should revise their curricula and programs and emphases on the basis of these central thoughts:

There are no interests functionally specialized which can be separated from the world striving, world need, world crisis.

Or in other words: isolationism is no longer possible. If we attempt it again, eventually war will push or pull us into global activity once more.

Or in still other words: No local community, no local group, can live significantly and register its citizenship if it does not consciously, responsibly decide to understand and to do something about those matters which are global and all-involving, and on which the fate of man itself depends.

There cannot be any satisfactory or even stable organization of world order, unless it be rooted in democratically responsible, globally oriented local communities whose leaders, at least, are linked to globally oriented national and international movements and associations. *Legacies and Inheritance Taxes*

The personality itself of the rising generation requires to be formed into the pattern of the world issues, the world hopes, and this forming of personality can only take place in the millions of local communities in which the young of the human race are educated and in which they form their attitudes.

These thoughts are obvious thoughts, but they certainly are thoughts that we do not live by. There is as yet no effort in the United States—nor in most other countries—to bring the world issues to the local community. We have not yet tried with skill and perseverance to bring the local community out into the world scope. A way should be sought to do this, to abolish the political and ideological vacuum in which most Americans now exist. Otherwise world and local chaos, local and world Fascism, world and local war will be certain to engulf us.

One World or No World—

Nothing else is worth worrying about. If we do

not work to crystallize ourselves internally so that we will be able to work effectively for the United Nations-One World idea with the ambition to make it succeed, there isn't very much use in doing anything else—not even digging deep holes way down in the ground in case one is curious about how the world will look after the next war, for "atomic gas" will seep into them too.

APPENDICES
AND NOTES

RESTATEMENT OF THE PASSAGE BACK IDEA

Parts of the letter mentioned at the beginning of Chapter 13 have been incorporated into Chapter 12; some of the rest reads as follows:

> Milford, New Jersey,
> January 25, 1942

Dear Mrs. Roosevelt: In *Two-Way Passage* I wanted to telescope—with focus on the current crisis—some of America's inner problems and resources not generally recognized; to examine her relationship to the rest of the world, particularly Europe; and to offer, for our collective thinking about the future, the Passage Back idea. The book was written in the summer of 1941. Your and the President's expressed interest in it prompts this post-Pearl Harbor restatement.

. . . It is not a blueprint, something finished, complete, rigid or dogmatic. In the book, I called it a suggestion. I hope it deserves to be called a generative idea; a scheme tossed out for discussion, something to be pulled apart, added to . . .

As of now [January 1942] my suggestion—*in its maximum form*—shapes up as follows:

In 1917, as part of its war effort, the United States Government—acting through its propaganda office, "the Creel Committee"—officially helped Thomas Masaryk, who already had strong moral and financial support from Czech and Slovak immigrants in this country, to organize *here* the government of Czechoslovakia. That state thus came into existence in Pittsburgh while its territory was still in Austria-Hungary, with which we were at war. This became a factor in Austria's collapse, in speeding the war's end, in the Allied-American victory. And I think it furthered the development of Czechoslovakia into one of the most democratic countries in Europe. Her system of government was patterned closely after ours; American influence there was always strong. Masaryk lived here for some years; his wife was an American; in the 1920's several Americanized Czechs and Slovaks returned to their native land to help its progress.

Now I propose that while Hitler still holds Europe—as soon as we can free ourselves of our "defense" mood and appeasement apparatus, and overcome our military inferiority; as soon as we are clearly on top of the heap—the United States Government, as part of our effort in this war, give purposeful, well-conceived official leadership to our immigrant groups, including refugees, in organizing *here* a continental European federation of national states. . . . Europe is a chief focus of the world problem. . . .

As a government, we are already planning to feed Europe after the war. And all sorts of schemes by private organizations to aid the Old World in other respects (health, education, economic reconstruction) are under way. All this will need to be co-ordinated; and I hope that this time, unlike in 1918-1920, we will have the sense to use food and other services not only to relieve immediate distress but also for immediate and long-range *progressive political purposes—to enhance the influence and power of the genuine democratic leaders who will appear, and to thwart their opponents.* After the last war, in many countries the Hoover relief organization helped the wrong people to entrench themselves in positions of authority.

I suggest that, carefully utilizing the human resources within our immigrant groups, we organize *here* American provisional or transitional governments or advisory groups or commissions which at the war's end would be prepared to take over, or assist in, the temporary direction of the European countries to be included in the Continental Federation, with one currency, an economic order that will work toward general welfare, one postal system, one trade and traffic control.

These governments or commissions or advisory groups (what we call them will not be the most important thing

246

about them) would be sent to Europe at the conclusion of hostilities, or before, and would stay there as long as needed. In taking temporary control, the scope of which would vary in different countries, they would have the support of special United States military units, and staffs of food distributors, doctors and nurses, engineers, teachers, educators and other experts—many of them immigrants and refugees from the countries to which they will return *as Americans in the service of the United States*; carefully selected volunteers, carefully trained for their functions and deeply impressed with the significance of their mission.

I propose that we take to Europe—in person—the American Revolution, the American Experience. . . .

On December 4 [1941] Secretary of the Interior Harold Ickes urged restoration of democratic governments or the establishment of such governments in countries which have never had a democratic order. "If necessary," he said, "we should impose democracy, just as a public health official imposes hygienic rules and regulations in civilized communities. . . ." Mr. Ickes comes close to my idea. But "impose" is not the right word. As I see the problem, the United States would not seek to impose democracy upon Europe from without; our function should be to cut loose the vicious tentacles of hate, narrow nationalism, oppression and frustration which lock up the inherent democracy that exists within the hearts of European peoples. They would themselves establish democracy throughout Europe—if they had the chance, if they could be released from the intricacies of their intra-European system; in a word, if they were free. All they need is a historic moment. We can help give it to them.

My proposal is that we take Europe into a kind of receivership for a time; into escrow. If we don't make too many mistakes, if our whole approach is honest, we will be trusted —not by the few in high places, to be sure, but certainly by the plain people of Europe—if our advance propaganda is well handled, if the executives in charge of the scheme are *utterly sincere and able to convince the people of the various countries of our sincerity. . . .*

There will be immense difficulties of course, here and abroad. Many routine diplomatic procedures, now sacred to our State Department and to foreign diplomats in Washington and to their governments, will have to be relegated to the past along with "defense" and appeasement and the rest of the red tape, hocus-pocus and general failure of our period. There will be opposition from the powerful who are often the least imaginative. . . .

Without some such idea, we here in the United States are apt to get into serious internal political snarls during the war and/or when the shooting ceases. . . .

Many observers have been too impressed by the abrupt unity we achieved on December 7, 1941. . . . The reflex is to "beat the pants off the Japs." This will not be sufficient for the long pull ahead. There is as yet no widespread feeling that the chief difficulty is in Europe. In fact, there is considerable resistance to that truth. Many elements of our recent confusion and disunity—analyzed in the first part of *Two-Way Passage*—still exist beneath the surface.

There are many weaknesses within us still which Nazi propaganda can exploit again. Too many of us are soft, addicted to comfort, looking for "the main chance" or "an easy way out." Too many of us still have no idea what this war is really about. Nearly all of us want to win it, but few know why. Most of us want to get it over with. This may be enough for the time being; it won't be in the long run. It could become a main reason for undesirable postwar developments at home and abroad.

There is our inherent escapism; our traditional isolationism. There is the passion for our respective "old countries," which in some cases serves as the basis for anti-Britishism. . . .

The aspects of our present unity which are superficial or negative need to be deepened, buttressed, made positive, so they will hold fast in the hard pull to carry us through our military victory *to the further victory of achieving a democratic future for ourselves and other peoples.*

. . . I have no way of knowing if the President means to use the idea. But I should like to say that much can be done . . . before we are ready to assume leadership. We should find people fit for important functions in the scheme. They will be useful even if the idea is not realized as fully as I should like to see it. They will be important when and if we invade Europe: when and if we send food and medical aid and other services to the countries from which many Americans stem.

I am afraid that once the war is "won," most Americans in the armed services will feel they have done the job; will want to return to their civilian life at home. But the job will be only half done; to finish it, we shall need *special* people, volunteers, who will commit themselves to winning the peace, and will submit to the necessary training. My mail evoked by *Two-Way Passage* suggests that such people are available.

The problem of the next peace is integral with this war. The view expressed here and there, that the job now is to win the war and nothing else, seems to me fallacious, dangerous. . . .

After the war is "won," the opportunity for a real reorganization of the world, for real peace, will last only a moment. A French proverb says: "God works in moments." And He usually needs help. . . .

COMMENTS ON TWO-WAY PASSAGE: *1941-1944*

From a New York woman, dated Dec. 7, 1941:

. . . I hate and fear fascism, and every measure the President has taken or attempted to take to combat this menace has been encouraging, at the same time that it has filled me with dread. This is because everything we are doing is obviously involving us more and more in the war, and no doubt eventually we will be completely involved, and war

seems futile if any victory which might be won is not going
to be a permanent victory for democracy. No such victory
can be gained unless concrete plans are made for after the
war. Military action without planning for the future beyond
hostilities seems futile. . . . *T-WP* is the first ray of light
I have seen on this problem.

The idea . . . of what could be accomplished by the
cooperation of American and European peoples is an
exciting one. Whether it will actually work or not needs a
prophet to say, but it is the first proposal that has been put
forth which gives due weight to the human element and
which might avert the reversion to the old game of power
politics. For that reason it is worth trying, and with the
full support of the American people there might be a possibility of success.

By the way, why limit the Passage Back to Europe? We
cannot live independently of China and Japan any more
than we can of Europe, or do you think that when Europe
straightens itself out the rest of the world will tend to do
the same?—

Then this P.S. dated December 21, 1941:

I had written the above when the news came of the
Japanese attack. In the excitement I pushed the letter aside
and now I cannot remember what more if anything I had
intended to say.

Now that we are fighting this war with guns and men as
well as supplies it is even more important to have some
assurance of the future beyond the fighting. Now we must
make sure that this is the last time. It is up to us, the people,
to see to this—to see that there is never again such a period
as followed 1918.

From an Ohio woman:

The idea will have to include a return to Japan from
Hawaii and the Pacific Coast! Of course there are some spies
and agents among the Japanese there, but I am *confident*
the great majority of them are loyal Americans and lovers
of democracy. I wish you would write something about their
mission to their "old country" after the war. From where

else will come the leaders of a new Japan which must appear when the militarists and their absurd Mikado are gotten rid of? . . . *(This part of the idea was taken up by Pearl Buck, and it was put into effect. Thousands of Japanese and Filipino Americans were trained for special wartime and postwar functions in the Pacific.)*

From a man in Minneapolis:

I was born and raised in England. I came to the United States in 1912 at the age of seventeen. From 1920 until recently I spent many years in Europe representing American firms. I had headquarters in London and traveled continuously in all countries. The subject of *T-WP* is consequently close to my heart. I heartily endorse the basic idea. But I think there will have to be a Passage Back also to England.

Americans generally look upon England as though it had the same outlook on life as they have. This is not so. In America one is born free and equal. In England one is born free but not equal. There is a tremendous difference between these two outlooks. . . . England needs democratic reform almost as much as Germany and others.

We have something in America not found anywhere else —at least not in so clear a form. Here the average kid in the street thinks and reasons for himself as no other kid does in all the rest of the world. It seems to me that it is our American job to take hold of the world and teach those lands from which we came the beauty of freedom as we know it . . . and I believe the rest of the world will turn to it with the same ease and unlabored motion as a flower turns to the light—provided of course we use our heads and put our best foot forward. . . .

From Hermann Hagedorn, writer, grandson of Friedrich Schwendler, a German immigrant and the founder of the fighting pro-Lincoln newspaper in the 1850's and '60's, Der New Yorker Demokrat:

. . . What you have in mind is possible. And apart from Czechoslovakia's birth as a nation in Pittsburgh in 1917,   251 there is something like a precedent in our own American history. When we defeated Spain in 1898, we took over Cuba, not for ourselves but as trustees for the Cuban people. The story has never been really appreciated by Americans as a whole, and the whole gallant episode has been almost forgotten. Under the influence of superficial, debunking historians, who have dismissed the whole Spanish War-and-Cuba episode with the words "romantic hysteria" and "sugar," the American people have never realized what a grand thing they did in Cuba. The Europeans never pretended to understand it at all. The thing looked so naïve.

This was it: We licked Spain, Cuba was ours by right of conquest. We were there, we governed the Island—awfully well, too!—and after four years we got out and turned the government over to the Cuban people. The story of the American provisional government of Cuba, under Leonard Wood as governor-general, is a magnificent story of selfless work on the part of one people in behalf of another. Wood had to build a nation out of the rag-tag ends of Spanish misrule, dramatized in mediaeval dungeons and concentration camps, to clean up a mess of plain and fancy filth, build roads and railroads, rid the island of disease (including yellow fever), teach the people the rudiments of popular government, of public education, of hygiene, of the care of the sick, the lepers, the insane. He had to get them on their feet economically . . . kid the radicals into line, and finally help them adopt a constitution and organize a government; do it all under pressure of American sugar people and partisan politicians, and just plain grafters.

That was Leonard Wood, but really it was America—America at her best, decently and honorably doing a job for which she has got no reward, and for which the Administration in power got no recognition in history.

We did that once and we can do it again. I can imagine moving into Germany and doing the sort of thing we did in Cuba. . . . One young American lieutenant, organizing the educational system of Cuba, another (now Major-General

Frank McCoy) at 22, drawing up the first budget for Cuba! And how they got after the American grafters when they tried to loot the Cuban post office! In some respects the venture would be easier in Germany than it was in Cuba. For one thing, we would not be dealing with a people largely illiterate and just out of peonage.

But there would have to be a lot of training of the individuals who were to go over. I'd like to see that training started now and have it include a freshening up of German on the tongues of those who would be the ones to go. Most Americans of German origin speak a pretty awful German, and the majority of the second generation don't speak it at all. I can see Columbia or Harvard or Washington University in St. Louis giving a special course in German history and institutions and another course in conversational German, for the training of the members of the provisional government and the hundreds of experts in various lines, the scientists, doctors, nurses, social workers, dietitians, journalists, radio commentators, etc., who would be required.

In addition, there would have to be another kind of training—the inspiration and dedication of all these as a kind of knighthood of freedom, an effort to help ordinary men and women to be bigger than they are, for the sake of America, of the old country and of all mankind. . . .

I don't think your idea is visionary. I think it is absolutely practical. Something like it worked in Cuba. Why not in Germany, Austria . . . ?

Leading editorial entitled "Two-Way Passage," June 8, 1942 Chicago Sun:

When a blight destroyed the vineyards of Europe in the 19th century, grapevine cuttings were sent from America. Hence we were able, so to speak, to give the Old Countries a transfusion.

Of course the American cuttings, had they been native to this soil, might not have flourished in Europe. But it so happened that they had come from Europe in the first instance and were therefore merely "going back home."

That human beings of European extraction could do as much was the theme of a recent book by Mr. Louis Adamic, an American writer who was born a Slovene in that fruitful corner of Central Europe which was then a part of the Austro-Hungarian empire and which became, in 1918, a part of Yugoslavia. The book, called *"Two-Way Passage,"* suggested that foreign-born Americans and their children, having developed their roots in the free soil of this country, now reverse the stream of emigration—go back to the lands of their ancestors and there teach the lessons of democracy and the better life.

The idea appealed to many Americans who, like Mr. Adamic, had their earliest roots in Europe. But the consensus seemed to be that few would be able to take advantage of it. Jobs were generally scarce in the Old Countries, and without a job, how could one support himself for an extended stay?

Circumstances appear to be on the point of removing this natural objection. It is now apparent that we shall have to feed Europe after the war. The tremendous task should be managed—doubtless will be managed—along the lines perfected by former President Hoover following World War I. That means that we shall have to send between 20,000 and 50,000 executives, field agents and others over there to distribute the food.

One may well inquire whether it would not make good sense to choose for the job men who speak one or more European languages, are familiar with the psychology of the people of one or more regions or countries and at the same time are thoroughly imbued with democratic principles and eager to pass them along to others.

The missionary value of such an undertaking can scarcely be exaggerated. Nor is there any doubt that such a group could be recruited from among those who . . . are anxious to go. Yet we must remember that even the most willing of volunteers would need training.

If there is any merit in the suggestion, now would seem to be the time to get going on the planning phase.

From a young man of 22 in Hartford, Conn.:

On my father's side I am a tenth-generation Yankee, while my mother was born in Scotland, having come to this country as an infant. . . . I attempt not to look with favor or disfavor on any individual merely because of his name or denomination.

Now let me try to give you my comments on *T-WP*. . . . First, I am to be drafted shortly, already having been classified; and I'd certainly hate to think that possibly hundreds of thousands of young Americans, fellows like myself, are probably going to be killed and that billions of dollars are going to be spent to eradicate this anti-human force of the Axis, *unless* it will result in a world which will be a better place to live in. It is certainly foolish to go all-out to defeat one system unless we have something better and concrete to offer in place of that system. Further, I agree with you when you say that we have that better system—Democracy. The task is to make it concrete for the rest of the world.

To our conservatives, a United States of Europe and a World Federation are Utopian ideas. My suggestion is to disregard them. Try to sell the idea to the younger generation, those of us who are the raw material of this future world-wide Democracy you want to see come into existence. . . .

From a senior at the University of Rochester:

The *T-WP* idea, I think, is essential to the future of Europe and the world. Professor Moore, of the U. of R., who is running for Congress this fall, also believes in it. And it seems to me that the American people in general are ready for some such scheme as you propose. All of us are beginning to realize that something drastic must be done to prevent these recurring wars which will destroy civilization if not prevented.

Democracy and freedom must be sold the world over in order to keep it safe here. But it is just at this point that the cause of the United Nations is weakest. We seem to be afraid to come out in the open for any daring plan that has any chance of success. We don't want to go back to the *status quo* and yet we are fearful of the future.

If the world is ever going to recover from this mess . . . the United States, because of its peculiar position, is going to have to be on fire with an idea of freedom for all mankind. We will of necessity have to sacrifice all else for this idea, including our vaunted standard of living. Can we rise to the occasion?

From Ohio:

I'm a woman who is growing old back here in the middle of the United States. With little to live on and that little so uncertain, I've felt particularly discouraged about my own apparent inability to do anything constructive in the present national and world situation. And I want you to know that *T-WP* has given me the first relief from that feeling of depression I have had.

I want to ask: When you get some definite plan going, could I give what money I might save for that purpose to help carry on the work? I can save a little from time to time, and eventually I might have a small sum I could give to help advance your idea. . . . I come of French, German, Scotch, Irish and English ancestry.

Our leaders in the government ought to be made to think and make their decisions on this basis: that all people everywhere, or nearly all, have hearts, all people have feelings, all people want good for their children.

From Washington, D. C.

I have just completed your book. Will say it is a beautiful cooking-up for the destruction of America. None of you foreigners can claim the right to the name of American, and print such books as yours. I was so mad by the time I got to the "suggestion" that I threw it clear across the room. . . . If no better use is made of this country that Washington fought for, and his soldiers bled for, to free us from the tyranny of England—to use our own resources and the blood of this country to finance and bleed for Europe every time they have a war—I think the sooner we cease to be *anything* the better for us all. . . . We need to be rid of the foreign element who have for some years been fomenting trouble here, and should have been kicked out long ago. It has reached a stage now where you don't dare do anything if you're a real American. However, we are going to have to begin to treat you like the vicious curs you are. You are abusing the freedom and protection this country's flag gives you. Most of you have starved and slaved in your wonderful "fatherlands." I visited Ellis Island many years ago when I was in New York, and have hated the name immigrant ever since. Look at the flock of Jews; they just walk in and cheat the eye teeth out of decent people. Then there are the foreign Communists, stirring up trouble with the niggers. God! when will we Americans wake up? . . .

From a wartime industrial worker at Long Beach, New York:

I want to tell you what a furor your book caused in the propeller room where I work at Grumann Aircraft. I took it to the plant one day to read during lunch hour. Joe, old-stock Scotch-Irish American, and Bill, German-ancestry American, smelled it, felt of it, and finally read the table of contents and pages here and there. On that day began a discussion which grows more interesting every day. Joe and Bill were anti-everything that suggests progress from a liberal point of view.

In the beginning, I felt it my role to expound, to declare, to preach the gospel of international understanding. They drowned me out, and then they listened, and now, at last, I have discovered that if I let them talk, they will talk themselves into a keener and sounder liberality than I could ever give them. It's funny. They surprise me, but they surprise themselves even more.

In this letter, and alone, I cannot think through to an articulate program of what should be done to introduce to other guys like Joe and Bill the ideas which you have presented. But the ground is rich, and God knows it has not even been spaded. And I am afraid that *T-WP* does not have much of a chance of catching their attention. And it is guys like Joe and Bill who ought to know about it. They are the mechanics, the riveters and welders, the assemblers, the carpenters, the floor-sweepers, who are winning this war and who ought to know what it is all about —but don't.

They don't read books. They don't read bulletins. They read the *News* and the *Mirror* and *Look* and *Life* and *Pic* and *True Detective*. And they talk—but in terms of the hopelessness of the world ever getting any better, of the inevitability of wars and more wars.

What can we do? If there were enough of us to go round, to filter into every unit of working men and women, and provoke arguments and leave copies of *T-WP* in conspicuous places, it would be good. Are there enough of us?

From John William Hughes:

You may be interested to know that your idea has clicked, not only in the minds of naturalized and second-generation Americans, but also in mine. I came over here from Europe in November 1938 for a three-month lecture tour, but the three months have been stretched to almost four years. . . . Having been a radio commentator from besieged Madrid, and an ambulance driver with the Loyalist forces in Spain, I came to lecture to the Americans about Europe, but stayed to lecture to them about their own country and its great possibilities; possibilities which are more obvious to a newcomer than to the American-born.

A short book of mine entitled *They Shall Not Perish* was published last February, and several people told me that your and my ideas were similar. I then read your book hastily, and drew upon it a good deal at a class on postwar reconstruction which I had in Missouri a few weeks ago. Yesterday I finished reading *T-WP* again, carefully this time. Today a batch of letters reached me from Great

Britain from people expressing agreement with my idea that leadership for the new Europe should come from the United States. One educationalist ordered 100 copies of the book. . . .

I am still a British subject, but being a Welshman I can look upon the European and the Imperial scene more dispassionately than an Englishman. . . . I have to get some lectures together, and with your permission I shall draw on your material.

I know that we in Wales never looked upon the United States as being foreign, because every family there has a part of it living here. I believe this is true of all European countries. Because of that, the masses of the people would welcome American leadership. Like yourself, I am very much afraid that the leadership given by the Governments-in-Exile would be leadership back, and I would be against shedding one drop of blood to rebuild the old Europe.

From a French refugee in Lisbon:

Two-Way Passage has for some time been discussed in Lisbon. Nearly everybody whom I know is agreed on this: the organization of Europe after the war will belong, if not completely, at least in large part, to America. News reaching us from the occupied countries is to the effect that the ruins caused by the war can be restored only by America; that the need for American leadership is inherent in and demanded by the situation. England having lost the confidence of Europe, and Russia being herself in ruins, America alone remains—America, the only country in whom Europe still holds an almost absolute faith.

Public opinion in occupied lands is also unanimous that Europe, all of Europe, after the war will necessarily be subject to social and economic changes as profound as radical, but that they must be given a democratic character. Doubt concerning the so-called governments-in-exile is general; as you underlined in your book, they cannot possibly play any part after the war.

But I have noticed with astonishment that—both in the

book and in the few bulletins which have reached me—you give no emphasis to refugees. You seem to ignore the fact that here in Portugal, as well as in the United States and elsewhere, in fact all over the Allied world, are hundreds and thousands of able men and women who have fled from their countries, who possess wide knowledge of European conditions and who could be used. Why not use them? Why not start training schools for them in America? Many will quickly learn American institutions and ways, which they can easily adapt and still more easily apply, once returned to liberated Europe.

Early in June 1942, Governor Harold E. Stassen spoke before the Northern Baptist Convention in Cleveland and advocated the "establishment of temporary governments over each of the Axis nations, preferably utilizing citizens of the United Nations whose ancestry goes back to the Axis nation involved." These temporary governments, said Stassen, who is of German-Norwegian-Czech ancestry, would "serve until a sound stabilized opportunity can be given for the people of a respective Axis nation to establish a proper government." (Sending me a copy of this speech, Stassen wrote: "I have read and re-read *Two-Way Passage*.")

News story in the July 20, 1943, New York Herald Tribune:

How a young Sicilian soldier captured a few minutes after the Americans pushed ashore at Gela on the south-central coast of Sicily was so overjoyed at meeting a former childhood comrade among the invaders that he led the Americans safely through mine fields and booby traps was described yesterday by a photographer who accompanied the landing forces.

Another unusual vignette of war was related by the photographer, Robert T. Landry, of *Life* magazine, who told how six men, speaking understandable English, were among the first group of civilians to greet the Americans at Gela. The men shouted jubilantly, "We from Brooklyn," and flung open their coats, pointing to the labels of Brooklyn stores where they had bought their clothes.

Mr. Landry and Norman Alley, a newsreel photographer who took 5,000 feet of film of the invasion, arrived at La-Guardia Field on an American Export Flying Ace. They were on one of the landing barges which rode the surf to the beach at Gela on July 10. On the barge with Mr. Landry and Mr. Alley was a small American soldier who had been chosen to act as interpreter.

The soldier, known to the photographers only as Harry, told Mr. Landry that his parents lived on a farm about ten miles from Gela. Harry said he had been reared there and that he had been brought to the United States eight years ago by an aunt and uncle. He did not know when he made this disclosure that he would be landing at Gela, but he hoped it would be somewhere near.

As the barges swarmed closer to shore Harry began to recognize landmarks and found it impossible to restrain his excitement. When the Americans landed the Sicilian soldiers began to surrender almost immediately. Even those who fired on the Americans "didn't take any too good aim," Mr. Alley put in. "They seemed to be expecting friends, or brothers or cousins, on the barges," he said.

Most of the prisoners were young and almost all wore new uniforms, suggesting that they had never been in battle before. Among them was a young corporal, the fuzz of adolescence still on his cheeks. He was taken before a group of officers, with Harry as interpreter.

After a few introductory questions, the flow of Italian became a torrent and in another moment Harry and the corporal were embracing each other. When the officers managed to tear Harry and the prisoner apart Harry explained that the corporal lived on a farm next to Harry's parents.

At the request of the officers, Harry then told the corporal that the Americans wanted to get over some hills and down to business, and asked the corporal if he would show the way. The corporal agreed and, Mr. Landry said, "running like hell, led us through the booby traps and minefields." Mr. Landry never did find out if Harry got to see his parents, but he presumed that there must have been a joyful reunion.

In every town the Americans took, Mr. Alley said, the civilians rushed out of houses to greet them, some of them waving American flags that they had kept hidden somewhere. It was a common sight to see American soldiers with Sicilian children on their knees, or drinking toasts of wine with townspeople.

"All in all," Mr. Landry said, "the landing was pretty much like old home week."

Columnist Marquis W. Childs visited liberated regions of Yugoslavia early in March 1944. On March 10 he wrote from Rome—in part:

This war is like a huge tapestry, with so much going on in the foreground and all of it so highly colored and exciting that extraordinary happenings in the background are overlooked. During my brief stay in Belgrade, I heard the story of one such background adventure from one of the participants.

Sgt. Carl W. Mitchell, now attached to the American military mission in Yugoslavia, was one of about 300 American enlisted men and officers who, in January, 1944, along with British Commandos, joined a band of Tito's Partisans on the island of Vis off the Dalmatian coast. Mitchell and the other Americans had been chosen from every branch of the armed services because they spoke one or another of the Slavic tongues. Thanks to his mother and grandparents, Mitchell speaks Serbo-Croatian. [Original family name Mihelich.]

When the group landed on Vis it was the only lifeline between that part of Italy held by the Allies and enemy-held Dalmatia. The assignment of the mixed force was to
harass enemy communications and create the utmost de-

struction and confusion by repeated Commando raids on the coast.

The first night, the whole camp was at a movie when the Germans, who had been tipped off by an agent on the island, staged an air raid. Fortunately, there were almost no casualties. From that moment on, there was never a dull moment.

The group made a landing on the Dalmatian coast, using Commando infiltration tactics, and stayed for three days near the town of Split. Immediately afterward, Mitchell, an American officer and a group of Partisans hid for six days in a cave on an island not far from Split. The Germans knew they were somewhere on the island and a patrol would have got them if it had not been for a warning given by a local boy. . . .

[But] of all the acts of sudden courage and heroism that became commonplace during the operations, Mitchell reserves his greatest admiration for that of Corp. George Kalitsis of New York, a Greek American who was born in Athens. Kalitsis, who wanted to go and fight for the liberation of Greece, never got a chance.

"He talked about it a lot," Mitchell says. "He really felt it, too. But on our very first mission we ran into a German ambush. They had us bad, and then Kalitsis stepped up to see a German mortar position. Well, he saw it, all right. They got him right in the head. But what it did was to give the Germans away and, if that hadn't happened, we would all have been killed, and that's true."

They took the body of Corp. Kalitsis back to the island of Vis. He was the first American to fall on Yugoslav soil. Sgt. Mitchell says the whole island gave him a funeral— the biggest funeral Mitchell ever saw.

Mitchell tells how the Americans learned to sing Partisan songs around the campfire. And then, one night, the Partisans surprised them. Without any help, they had learned "Stars and Stripes Forever. . . ."

"They're wonderful fighters," Mitchell says. "You never saw any fighters like them. They'd do everything they could

263

to protect us. They'd give a hundred lives for one American life."

Finally, the job on the Dalmatian coast was completed and it was time to leave the base on Vis. The entire population came to see the group off.

"We all bawled like a bunch of babies," says Mitchell. "They bawled and we bawled and—well, you never saw any people like that."

Most of the group went off to fight in Greece with the Greek guerilla bands in the mountains. That was something, too, but you can tell from the way Mitchell talks that, for him, nothing will ever equal that period of wild life on the Dalmatian coast.

This is the story of a boy who comes from South Honore St. in Chicago. He tells it without any trimmings at all, but you know he understood the full meaning of what he saw. He and those who came out of the assignment with him will never forget the quality of life among the peasants of Dalmatia. I would guess that the Dalmatians also learned a lot about America and Americans.

Louis Adamic once wrote a book urging that Americans of foreign descent be sent back to their respective homelands as a way to bring about real understanding. Maybe he was right. Maybe the response of young Americans like Sgt. Mitchell proves something. I have a feeling that it will last longer than anything politicians may do.

From a Missourian (August 1943):

Politically, the war has about lost all meaning except in the worst aspects. Churchill is the reason, of course. He has emerged top-dog and F.D.R. appears to be his willing stooge. Churchill is a great man, indeed; but only a salvage expert. He has no more interest in the future than a rabbit —no concern about the shape-up of tomorrow, just so it's the same shape it was last night. A great, quiet struggle for control of the postwar world has developed between Churchill, backed by F.D.R., and Stalin. Stalin will win, not merely because he's right, but because he has always been a conscious architect of society and has become infinitely trained and shrewd in that art. The cards all lean his way because Europe is conditioned for real change or will be by the time the war is over. Churchill is doing his utmost to prevent change, to reestablish the old Europe, and he hasn't a chance of ultimate success. He may score temporarily, but it will just mean more bloodshed and violence before Europe finds its level.

Stalin's victory will not mean his walking off with Europe. Far from it! But it will consist in preventing Churchill from prevailing. For only a free Europe will secure Russia. Everyone knows that Churchill privately hates Russia's government and wants to bring about its fall; he rightly fears that its maintenance, on top of the enormous prestige it will have gained in the war, will result in far-reaching alterations in the social-economic setup of the British Empire. . . . Europe will go socialist with half a chance, and that will be okay with Stalin; for even a non-Stalinist socialist Europe would end the Continental menace to the USSR, and constitute, by so much, a great victory for Uncle Joe.

You've got to admire the quiet, slick, patient and shrewd way Churchill has finagled F.D.R. into his hands! He's just about displaced him in popularity in the United States even.

We needed Churchill—he was the man for the job; but what a lot of mischief he is capable of in the postwar world! That talk he gave out the other day is merely dynamite. We *can't* start off with an exclusive alliance be-between Britain and the United States. It would not only foment other alliances, racial and of mutual interest for self-protection against us—China, Japan, India and Russia, Germany, France—but there could be no hope of Britain and the United States alone maintaining peace in the world. It would break the backs of the tax-payers, and we'd sabotage it just about the time we had succeeded in arousing some hostile, jealous combination against us.

No. Any exclusive "English-speaking alliance" is the

last thing we want. The time is long gone when an open alliance based on same-color or same-speech might have been effective. The world has become too much the same. It is, indeed, One World, because it now operates by a single principle: similar means of existence, *i.e.*, industrialism. The Japanese, Chinese or Hindus will have the means to make modern engines of war as well and plentifully as the western "English-speakers."

The essential tragedy is the universal adoption of the idiotic doctrine that only force will maintain peace henceforth. All countries have gone hog-wild over that doctrine, and all are thinking of rebuilding the postwar world upon it as the cornerstone. It is the rottenest lie yet produced, and the essential reason why the present war is only a starter for another.

We're all going to pay plenty for this idiocy—and chaos and even anarchy will be the logical end-products. Simple. Sufficient armaments nowadays [letter written two years before the atomic bomb dropped on Hiroshima] are so costly that people will find themselves paying four bits out of every buck just to "keep the peace." They'll begin to kick and rage, and in the long run they'll probably decide that it's actually cheaper to cut armaments way down and take our chances, and go all out for war expenses when the real threat of war actually comes. So—we're headed for the same old stupid tail-chasing round again. Because we have not got leaders great and courageous enough to inspire and electrify the people of the world into a genuine effort at vitally needed reform.

Churchill says we'll open a second front when we're ready, but we don't do it "for political reasons." I'd like to know what better reason there could be for such a great effort than *political* reasons. Seems to me that is just what is wrong with us—we're doing everything for little two-bit, pinch-penny "realistic" reasons, and thereby spending our blood and wealth to buy only the thing we had before. . . . Isn't it about time we had the courage and greatness to match our physical effort and sacrifice with at least one great "political" effort, for the greatest possible *political* ideals? Isn't this war about *politics* too—to keep Hitler's brand away from us and to re-make the world so as to prevent its resurrection at least for a long time? The issue is in the sad, grim, purblind, stubborn attitude of Churchill and F.D.R.—the penny-ante way they handled the French Committee, the wiggling and gesticulating about Italy, the quaking, ghost-seeing terror about "anarchy" in Italy. What's wrong with us? I know we are a stupid and backward people when it comes to international politics, but we are not *that* trivial and cheap. Churchill and F.D.R. have let us all down by playing us and our great potentialities too close to their vests.

It is quite clear that England has called the tune and we've followed. For this is not the American way at all! There's still a lot of the old reckless, daring, take-a-chance spirit in America and it would assert itself well if given the chance. But Churchill has captured it and funneled it through the narrow, devious Empire-politics system. We've welded ourselves irretrievably to an obsolescent British Empire that is held together only by the blood and sweat of our combined countries, and that will fall apart soon after the war ends. And then we'll pay the price, we'll be isolated. Politically, Europe and the postwar world are lost, and we all know it—Europe knows it—*Stalin knows it.*

Obviously, the only hope would be a strong, all-out alliance, at once, between Britain, China, Russia and us, and anyone else who cared to join with our common aims. It must be either that or nothing. There are no longer possibilities for successful partial alliances, or geographical or racial ones.

When one thinks of Churchill's great qualities . . . one despairs that he is so short of measure in other ways—above all in *vision*, and some concept of what mankind has yearned for inarticulately for 25 years. With only a few—yet major—concessions he could have the whole world behind him. But politically he remains a little man—and always, when the chips are down, an "islander" and an

267

English Tory. Had he been a master world-statesman, he'd have had millions of Indians to help us fight the Japs.

Stalin will defeat him, but one thinks of that conflict with sadness. The world has to go through more needless shock, revolt, suffering and chaos, owing to Churchill's faults and stubbornness, and F.D.R.'s inadequacy—*which is our national inadequacy*. And it seems that Churchill is playing even his small-town brand of politics very doubtfully. Is he unaware of the depth of Russian popularity in Britain? . . .

It is clear, however, that the struggle for Europe that began as a battle between Stalin and Hitler has shifted. It has become virtually a struggle for the world, *and Churchill has assumed the declining Hitler's role*.

But Stalin is already winning. This is shown in the peremptory or indifferent attitude he shows toward both Churchill and F.D.R., whereas they bow and scrape and make almost embarrassing public apologies to him. He has only to make a little growl and they flutter about in anxious supplication and fright. This is eloquent enough of the lousy political situation into which our two countries have got. It is *humiliating*.

As for the alibi about the necessity of "winning the war" —what platitudes we've been drenched with, in the place of commonsense facts! How naïve and childish we've become! . . .

From a Mid-Western college professor:

I want to get a few things off my chest. . . . I do not fear the "masses," the Great Unwashed. But slowly for years, since I became a college prof., I have come to have a shuddering fear of what is now my own class. They are never brutal, they are too fearful of everything and everybody to be anything but polite and ineffective. Their very supineness is what I fear. They are truly the unleavened mass, and they cannot be leavened. I am no statistician and I do not know how they count up in the total population, but if they add up to a substantial number, even if not a

268

majority, then God pity us; God pity this country. This is not the unstudied reaction of a savage who graduated into the white-collar class, but a judgment gradually forced upon me by 30 years of association with people who crawl instead of walk, who whisper instead of talk, who calculate and weigh the social and financial advantage of every move before they dare to make it.

All through the years as an escape from the society of such people I have often foregathered with Italians and Greeks and Frenchmen and a few Hindus, and China-boys, and Russian Jews, and German Jews and Jewesses. I did that as a relief without rationalizing my behavior. But since I have learned to think I have studied the behavior of the white-collared class, the paper-workers, the brass-collars. They simply cannot see beyond their own little shaved lawns. Even those who, like myself, fear the political reactionaries, will do nothing about it—but vote—for fear of losing their jobs. This fear of the job is a terrible thing; it makes us worse slaves than any of the so-called wage-slaves. You see, we are documented from job to job, our record kept down to date, our past always subject to scrutiny. I tried to break out by becoming a freelance writer, and I damn' near starved. You see, I am confessing that I am one of this frightened crowd; but I can't break out; I have too many domestic obligations. Free in mind, I am bound hand-and-foot in speech and behavior. Don't believe the stories you hear about academic freedom; it doesn't exist, not even in our biggest universities. I know.

Now, I have always known that politicians were bad and that politics stank, and like most idealists I have had and worked at schemes for making it cleaner. But never till Chamberlain and Daladier sold the Czechs down the river, after having sold the Spanish Republicans down river, did I realize that a people are helpless at any given moment, like emigrant passengers closed under hatches or passengers in an airplane, in the hands of the political group that happens to be in the saddle. I was dumb in matters of political science and never realized it till its terrible lessons came home to me from Spain and Czechoslovakia, and most terrible of all from France and from your native country, Yugoslavia. Now, since I have children and grandchildren, the idea of what politicians, so-called statesmen, can do, simply frightens me stiff. I may or may not admire Roosevelt; but he has *too damn' much power*—and Congress, *too damn' much power*—and Churchill, *too damn' much power*. . . .

For two years now I have been eating and drinking at a little hamburger joint where laboring men foregather. I've had my eyes opened. They're not the scum of the earth, they're the cream of the earth. They are not afraid of their jobs; they can get others. There is more of the gambler in them. Their imaginations are not so refined and full of nuances as those of my white-collared class. They were the first to condemn America First. But as they get up the scale, more skilled, nearer the white-collars, they become conservative, more careful in speech and action—more to lose, a home being paid for, boys and girls in college. I could tell anybody, a college education isn't worth it. They sell their souls for a little social and economic gain. And it is little, oh, so little. Had I remained a house painter, I could at least have wangled votes for the causes I believe in; as it is I dare not. I hardly dare admit I voted for Roosevelt. I am simply not a man, but a salary-earning automaton, dealing in split infinitives and lost antecedents.

This would be no tragedy if there were only a few of us; but there are hundreds of thousands, and if you start counting in bank clerks and small tradesmen of all sorts it runs into millions. Millions who cannot see the good of the whole, but can think only in terms of themselves and their families. And let me tell you, your second- and third-generation ex-Europeans, especially Germans, are the very worst of the lot. You can get an Irish American to pop off, not a German American, or a Swedish American or a Danish American; not after he gets a good job. Perhaps the poor devil remembers his grandfather's tales too vividly.

I have starved—a little—it wasn't bad. I have tramped

and begged for hand-outs; it wasn't bad at all. I could do it again. But my wife and daughters and grandchildren are a different matter. Don't think I am just blowing my top. This is a cold-blooded report of the part of the American scene I have witnessed at close range. I have tried hard to observe and reason things out. I have been at banquets and been sick and disgusted but of course made no sign by word or gesture; then I have said to myself: "Perhaps a fourth or a third or more than half of these people feel just as I do." But when over a long period of years every chance remark I have made to the effect that things were not just as they should be has always drawn a noncommittal reply or an open denial of my thesis, I have to conclude that these people think the way they talk. Of course I know that most people are mentally very lazy and will not exercise their brains except for practical purposes; but I still have to attribute the inanity of the white-collar class to fear rather than to mental laziness. They have taken the line of safe practice and walked in it till it has become second nature.

But there is hope in our young people; they can see the feebleness of my generation, can see how little we have got by our cowardice. Things are better, more liberal, around our colleges than they were even ten years ago, and of a different complexion altogether from what they were 20 years ago. Then "leadership," "salesmanship," "showmanship," was everything; today there is far more honesty, far more smouldering rebellion. . . .

From a young woman in Los Angeles:

. . . We are involved in a shift in environments and a shift in values.

We now discover that each individual must budget his attention to express his interests in the world, the nation, the community, his friends, his family and himself. He must establish habitual action in all of these relationships or be as truly crippled as if he denied some of the relationships of his own body.

People didn't do that. Their world was small enough for

automatic and unconscious integration. Since 1918 our old
integrations have split. Since 1930 they have been tenta-
tively re-formed and re-expressed, but in this war we will
articulate techniques and relationships in terms of all our
environments for all types of individuals. We cannot depend on unconscious integration. We must figure out many
reciprocal relationships, try them out, and discard those that
don't work.

Politically, we oppose the totalitarian belief that all the
world must conform to one pattern, with the need and the
ability to establish techniques of co-ordinating conflicting
ways of living, each of which is good within the limits of its
own geography and history. Democracy is one of these techniques. We need to learn others. We will teach totalitarian
people that other nations and races are also good by working *with* them on tangible aims. We must display our
strengths (and have strengths to display) in unmistakable
forms—by our versatility, our physical and mental resiliency,
our spiritual adequacy, our physical vigor, and above all by
our gaiety. We will teach them that the independent
abilities of each group are necessary to each of the others
for their stimulation and their enjoyment.

Economically, we are abandoning the myth that any one
economic technique should or does in fact exclude others.
We must learn and we must teach that reciprocity in trade
and investment is superior in benefits to the geographic
units involved than a position of either creditor or debtor
nation. We must develop new techniques of exchange and
distribution, separately and together.

Philosophically, we realize that most dilemmas are self-
imposed. The totalitarian states operating on the belief
that what is not identical with them is therefore hostile to
them will be taught the concept of multiple values—that
ours is a universe of many entities, purposes, processes,
and materials, any one of which may or may not be relevant
to the welfare of each of the others. This is not a world of
black and white, but one of many lovely shades and colors—
and sounds, odors, and other pleasant things. We know that

272

no relationship can be good nor permanent unless it works both ways. He who gives must receive, and he who receives must give—but not on his own terms nor at his own convenience. Nor can any abstraction be of value unless it is translated in specific actions in specific circumstances.

Socially, we recognize the validity of other customs for other people. We presume that the individuals we meet are our equals and may quite possibly show themselves to be our superiors in ways that we value. We know that we must give each person we meet our individual attention, our respect for his integrity, and our expressed appreciation of his merits, be he Jew, or German, or Jap. If we do not give these things, we have no claim to his tolerance or his consideration.

Spiritually, I am no longer the center of the universe. I shall never know all about anything, nor shall I ever be certain that my actions will be the best possible solution of any problem. But in spite of my limitations, the responsibility for a decent world is mine. If other people are to stand firm against evil, I must use my own courage and risk my own losses. I must see and use every opportunity to create. If God is to exist, it must be through my actions, multiplied by the actions of a million other people. Only by this means can better things come.

A LETTER TO OSS

On August, 2, 1944, I wrote to Mr. David Williamson of the Office of Strategic Services in Washington—in part:

Referring to our conversation in your office on July 26 about my availability for work within your organization in Yugoslavia: I am eager to be used and will make myself available if the OSS wants me after considering the ensuing paragraphs.

1. It has been my conviction since early in 1943 that the postwar developments in Yugoslavia—in all of Yugoslavia, including Serbia—will issue mainly from the People's

Liberation Movement under Tito's leadership, and that the only sound basis for an American attitude or policy toward Yugoslavia would be a full acceptance of the desirability of such developments. But for the organization and the political, moral and spiritual dynamics created by the Partisans' resistance against the enemy, the Yugoslav problem would now be utterly unmanageable.

For too long this was not the basis of our official thinking about Yugoslavia. I don't know that it is yet. As recently as two months ago some of our officers in Cairo and Bari were openly unfriendly to the Partisans; they may still be.

American prestige was always great in the Balkans. Our prolonged reluctance to accept the Tito movement has damaged that prestige, but not irreparably. I believe it can be made greater than it was before 1942-44, and that the groundwork for a constructive long-range relationship between the United States and Yugoslavia can be laid. I am more than ready to help in this. But I shall be able to help effectively as a member of your organization, attached to the staff of the American general commanding in Yugoslavia (which you suggested might be the assignment), only if our official attitude toward the new Yugoslavia has changed or is changing. I don't see how I could function under superiors antagonistic to the Tito development, or reluctant to accept it and work with it in a constructive way.

The point is: if we have not accepted or are not beginning to accept the desirability of what has happened there, my usefulness in Yugoslavia would not be likely to amount to much and I think it would be better to leave me here. If we are beginning to accept it, then I can probably become useful and, as I say, I am eager to be sent over.

2. I feel it would be an error to send me to Yugoslavia and inhibit me as a writer. If I am well regarded there, it is because I wrote two books about the country and served as president of the United Committee of South-Slavic Americans from June 1943 to April 1944. My views on the recent process in Yugoslavia are a matter of public

record. Tito and other leaders have read my books. Should I be sent there, it might be assumed that I had come precisely because of what I had written and that the United States accepted developments there. On the other hand, if I should not be able to express myself along the line of my known views and ideas, I might readily become an object of suspicion and the motives of the United States government in bringing me might also be questioned.

Besides, my chief medium of work and expression is writing, and curtailing it would curtail my usefulness.

Were I sent to Bari, say, within the next month or two, and from there to Yugoslavia as soon as possible, I might be able to do a good deal by talking with people, especially with the new national and local leaders, many of whom I know from my visit there in 1932-33, and many of the rest of whom know of me; by being helpful to them, writing for their press, visiting their institutions, attending their meetings and congresses; by writing about the developments in Yugoslavia for American publications and then having some of these articles translated into Yugoslav languages; by spotting and interpreting trends and conditions to, and being generally cooperative with, the responsible American officers and officials in Yugoslavia.

I will have an advantageous position with the Yugoslavs. They will talk with me freely, tell me things they would not reveal to many other people. I will want to be careful not to abuse their confidence. As a general rule, I will not want to be an informer on persons, but on important conditions, situations, developments, tendencies. I will consider it my duty to inform my superiors only of individuals and groups dangerous to the interests and purposes of the United States and the recognized setup in Yugoslavia.

I can hope to achieve something only if I am trusted by both my fellow Americans in Yugoslavia and by the Yugoslavs themselves. . . .

3. In our conversation, a reference was made to my "leftism." Labels mean various things to various people;

I generally dislike them. Lots of persons, including some in Washington, seem to think that "leftist" means violent, treacherous subversiveness. If the label is to be applied to me, I accept it along with the classic meaning of *Left*— "those holding relatively liberal or democratic opinions" (Oxford Dictionary). My guess is that I should be sent to Yugoslavia because I am a "leftist" of this definition and a member of several American organizations aiming to promote general welfare, respect for minorities, and other democratic concepts and aspirations.

ACKNOWLEDGMENTS

During the writing and proofreading I had the help of my wife Stella and my assistants Isabel Mangold and Ellen Ruth Seacat. Mrs. Ethel H. Sharpe of Milford, New Jersey, helped with the typing.

Set in Linotype Baskerville
Format by A. W. Rushmore
Manufactured by The Haddon Craftsmen
Published by Harper & Brothers
New York and London